The (

On the Road Guide to Taking Pounds Off

Terry Riley, Ph.D.

The Complete Travel Diet

On the Road Guide to Taking Pounds Off

Terry Riley, Ph.D.

Applied Psychology Press
Santa Cruz, California
USA
www.AppliedPsychology.com
www.CompleteTravelDiet.com

Copyright © 2004 Terry Riley

All rights reserved. No part of this guide may be reproduced or transmitted in any form or by any means, electronic or mechanical, including photocopying, recording, or by any storage and retrieval system, without express written permission from the publisher. If you violate our copyright, we may or may not sue you, but we will most definitely be pissed off.

Published by: Applied Psychology Press
22 Rincon Court / West
Santa Cruz, California 95060-1016 USA
Editorial office: +1-831-439-0922
Order desk (USA): 800-492-5050
E-mail: press@appliedpsychology.com

ISBN 0-9642698-4-8

Cover photograph by Bob Pilatos, rlpilatos@earthlink.net

Printed in the United States of America

To Linda
My complete traveling companion.

Contents

Forward 1

1. A TRAVEL DIET? 3
   The Complete Travel Diet's secret formula 4
   What The Complete Travel Diet *cannot* do 7
   What The Complete Travel Diet *can* do 7
   Your chance of success: The bad news 8
   Your chance of success: The good news 8
   Your safety 9
   Using this guide 10

2. TAKING STOCK 11
   Your fitness level 12
   Your Calorie needs 15

3. GOALS AND PLANS 19
   Goals 20
   Plans 21
   Follow through 25

4. NUTRITION 27
   Carbohydrates 28
   Proteins 30
   Fats 31
   Fiber 34
   Vitamins 35
   Minerals 35
   Water 35

5. **DIET** 37
    Calories 38
    Food Guide Pyramid 40
    Servings and portions 50
    Terms 59
    Meal replacements 62
    Supplements 63
    Medications 64
    Eating habits 64

6. **ACTIVITY** 69
    How exercise burns Calories 71
    Keys to being active 72

7. **ATTITUDE** 75
    Getting Started 76
    Continuing 81

8. **MODEL PLANS** 97
    Case one: Traveling businesswomen 98
    Case two: Vacationing men 116
    Case study synopses 134
    For vegetarians 137

9. **TRAVEL TIPS** 139
    Safety and security 140
    Before you go 140
    Transportation 153
    Lodging 156
    Restaurants 160
    Restaurant style 164
    Returning home 178

10. **RESOURCES** 181

    INDEX 185

Forward

I'm very pleased with this book... but not very pleased with its title. The information I have assembled is not just about dieting while "on the road." It's about maintaining or even improving your health and level of fitness while traveling. And although diet plays a major role in this objective, it is far from the only component that contributes to your health and fitness. Frankly, I would have preferred a title such as, "Information and Advice That Can Help You Maintain or Achieve Better Health and Fitness While You Are Traveling and After You Return."

But you can see the problem. That title isn't catchy enough for publication, and it would probably need a disclaimer to prevent some nincompoop from suing me because my "advice" didn't work. So although the title is not altogether inappropriate, I want to make it clear that there is more to THE COMPLETE TRAVEL DIET than monitoring and moderating your food intake. Just as important are changes in your level of physical activity and your attitude.

Together these three factors—diet, exercise, and attitude—represent a change in lifestyle. That's what THE COMPLETE TRAVEL DIET is all about: Changing your habits while you are away from home, then incorporating those lifestyle changes back into your routine once you return from your trip.

In compiling THE COMPLETE TRAVEL DIET, I found that reliable information about weight loss is evolving and incomplete. For instance, little is known about the role of your genetic disposition to gaining, losing, or maintaining body weight. In other cases, reliable information about weight loss is not without some differences of opinion among researchers and practicing nutritionists and physicians. For instance, there are differences of opinion about changes in metabolic rate as a

The Complete Travel Diet

function of time of day. And there is considerable disagreement about the relative proportion of Calories that should come from eating carbohydrates, proteins, and fats.

Nevertheless, from this incomplete knowledge base of weight loss and maintenance, I've done my best to provide accurate and useful information to help you control your weight while vacationing or traveling on business. The advice I offer up, however, is just that: Advice. It should not take the place of common sense. It is your responsibility to apply the advice in a manner that is appropriate to your particular health conditions and traveling situations.

Have a wonderful and healthful trip.

Terry Riley, Ph.D.
Santa Cruz, California, USA

ONE

A travel diet?

Travel and diet

"Travel" and "diet" may seem incompatible. Thoughts of dining on lettuce and cottage cheese while others at a business dinner or a captain's buffet are raving about the food may be too much to bear. A "travel diet" may seem oxymoronic—or simply moronic—especially when traveling for leisure.

Most people think that being away from home—either on vacation or on business—is no time to try to change their behaviors. Indeed, many see travel as an occasion to abandon a healthy lifestyle. They tend to partake in eating less wholesome food (and more of it), and they engage in less active behaviors. Indeed, many people leave on their trips with an *expectation* of gaining weight!

THE COMPLETE TRAVEL DIET

In the face of the popular notion that traveling and dieting are incompatible, why should you even consider following THE COMPLETE TRAVEL DIET?

There are two reasons:

ONE: If you are on a weight loss or maintenance program while at home, why would you want to put at risk what you have already accomplished? THE COMPLETE TRAVEL DIET will help you continue your program.

TWO: If you are putting off beginning a weight loss or maintenance program, traveling may be the best time to start. Because travel often interferes with your normal routines—including your unhealthy routines—there may be no better time to introduce changes in behavior.

That's not to say that losing weight or maintaining it while traveling will be easy. Behavioral change is challenging, and lifestyle changes are among the most difficult to make because they involve so many adjustments, from the way you act to the way you think.

From improving your health to improving your appearance, there are as many reasons to lose weight as you have pounds to lose. Whatever your reasons to lose weight, the information and tips in this book will help you achieve that weight loss and enjoy the consequent benefits you will surely gain.

The Complete Travel Diet's secret formula

Right here at the beginning, I'll let you in on THE COMPLETE TRAVEL DIET's secret formula for losing weight while on leisure or business travel. Ready? Here it is: Eat a little less, and move a little more. That's it. This simple maxim is the es-

A TRAVEL DIET?

sence of what you will read in the following pages. I won't belabor these points, but I will reinforce them.

"Ah, but that's exactly the problem with traveling," you say. "I eat too much, and I move too little."

Well, that sure is easy to do when traveling, but so is the alternative. Indeed, travel offers just as many opportunities to eat less as to eat more, and it almost always offers more opportunities to move more rather than less.

This sounds simple, and it is. But it isn't easy—particularly for travelers. It isn't easy because it requires changing habits, changing routines, and changing the way you are used to traveling. But it doesn't change the truth about weight loss: To lose weight—and to keep that weight off—you must burn more Calories than you eat.

THE COMPLETE TRAVEL DIET offers you a chance to make some real and lasting lifestyle changes that can result in the loss of a pound or two while you are on your trip. But more importantly, it will allow you to lose several pounds over the next few months if you integrate those new behaviors into your lifestyle at home.

THE COMPLETE TRAVEL DIET has been developed to be easily incorporated into your travel routines without interfering with your leisure or business activities. Its key elements are simplicity, adaptability, and flexibility.

Simplicity

Any complex regimen that makes it difficult to keep track of what, when, and how much you should eat and exercise will soon prove too cumbersome to follow. Eventually a complex system is likely to be abandoned—particularly when you are trying to conduct business on the road or enjoy your vacation.

THE COMPLETE TRAVEL DIET

So THE COMPLETE TRAVEL DIET sacrifices some accuracy for simplicity. It does not require you to eat or delete specific food items from your diet nor partake in any particular activity. Moreover, there is no intricate system of accounting for each and every Calorie you ingest or burn. THE COMPLETE TRAVEL DIET is an imprecise system that focuses on general behaviors of eating and exercising. THE COMPLETE TRAVEL DIET is intended to be easy to follow at the expense of being precise.

As you will read, THE COMPLETE TRAVEL DIET is a simple system of accounting. On the intake side, you need only to keep track of the number of servings you consume from each of six general food groups. And on the output side, you need only to account for the minutes you partake in an activity.

Again, these need only to be approximations. If you are a little off here and there, it is not a crisis. The idea is to keep your Caloric input within a certain range and your Caloric output above a certain threshold.

Adaptability

Travel can take you to places where the foods are different, are prepared in different manners, and are served at different times. These differences are, in fact, what can make travel such an enriching experience. And in keeping with these differences, THE COMPLETE TRAVEL DIET has been developed to accommodate a trip to almost anywhere at anytime.

Flexibility

The rigors and uncertainties of travel can easily derail a diet or exercise plan that requires strict adherence. THE COMPLETE TRAVEL DIET allows for the uncertainties of travel by not requiring the consumption of specific foods, the participation in specific activities, or the timing of specific behaviors.

A TRAVEL DIET?

Other than the watchwords of variety, moderation, and balance in your diet and physical activities, there are no restrictions on the foods you may eat or the activities in which you may engage. Indeed, adaptability of THE COMPLETE TRAVEL DIET makes it easy to get started, easy to follow while traveling, and easy to transition back into a healthful eating and exercise routine after returning home.

What The Complete Travel Diet *cannot* do for you

Before I tell you what THE COMPLETE TRAVEL DIET *can* do for you—and so that you aren't expecting too much—let me tell you what THE COMPLETE TRAVEL DIET *cannot* do for you.

THE COMPLETE TRAVEL DIET cannot transform you into a supermodel or give you rock hard abs (unless, of course, you are already drop-dead gorgeous or are just one sit-up away from a washboard tummy). THE COMPLETE TRAVEL DIET cannot make you smell better or more popular with the opposite sex. THE COMPLETE TRAVEL DIET cannot make you smarter, a better driver, or a lottery winner. Most relevant, THE COMPLETE TRAVEL DIET cannot "melt off pounds while you sleep" or help you "lose ten pounds by this weekend." Sorry.

What The Complete Travel Diet *can* do for you

On the other hand, THE COMPLETE TRAVEL DIET can help you maintain your weight or even drop a couple of pounds while on vacation or on a business trip. This will in turn enhance your traveling experience. You'll sleep better. You'll have more energy. You'll have less stress. And you'll feel better about yourself.

Your chance of success: The bad news

Chances are that this is not the first diet book you have purchased. And chances are—if you fit the norm—it won't be the last. Indeed, it can be stated with "near certainty" that statistically, you will not succeed at dieting. I realize that this is hardly the motivational pep-talk you need at this juncture—not to mention that this kind of statement does little to increase the sales of this book—but it's the truth. You know it. I know it. All diet "experts" know it. But...

Your chance of success: The good news

"Near certainty" is not absolute certainty. There will be a number of people who will follow the advice offered here and will not only lose weight while traveling, but they will make important changes in their lives when they return home so that they will continue to lose weight and will succeed in maintaining that weight loss.

If you set realistic goals, if you are motivated, and if you are disciplined, you can be one of these success stories. By losing excess weight through a healthy diet and regular exercise, you will improve your appearance, increase your self-esteem, and decrease the probability that you will suffer from depression. Moreover, you will reduce your risk of developing heart disease, stroke, type 2 diabetes, certain forms of cancer, gall bladder disease, osteoarthritis, high blood pressure, and sleep apnea. Losing even small amounts of weight (five to ten percent of your body weight), may reduce these risks. You may add years to your life while at the same time improving the quality of your remaining years.

A TRAVEL DIET?

At first you may find THE COMPLETE TRAVEL DIET to be a little awkward and inconvenient. However, any inelegances or inconveniences that you may experience are minor compared to the risks of overweight and obesity.

Your safety

There is risk involved with changes to your lifestyle. Before undertaking any change to your diet or exercise routine, get a checkup from your doctor. Weigh the advice offered here with that of your physician and a dietetics professional such as a registered dietitian. Then apply THE COMPLETE TRAVEL DIET as you and they see fit. No information in THE COMPLETE TRAVEL DIET is intended to medically diagnose or advise.

THE COMPLETE TRAVEL DIET has been designed to promote weight loss of no more than two pounds—or one percent of total body weight—per week. Medical authorities recommend that losing weight at such a rate reduces the risk of health problems that have been associated with more rapid weight loss (greater than three pounds per week). While traveling, you may lose weight at a slightly higher rate. So monitor your progress and modify your diet if your rate of weight loss after the first two or three weeks exceeds a rate of three pounds (or one and one-half percent of body weight) per week.

Children and adolescents, pregnant or breast feeding women, people on special diets or regimens of activity, and people with significant health problems such as bulimia, heart disease, kidney disease, diabetes or psychiatric disorder, should not begin THE COMPLETE TRAVEL DIET without authorization by their primary care provider. If you are under treatment for other conditions or taking medications prescribed by your health care provider, you should tell your provider that you have begun THE COMPLETE TRAVEL DIET because, in some cases, adjustments to

THE COMPLETE TRAVEL DIET

medications or modifications to THE COMPLETE TRAVEL DIET may be appropriate.

Weight loss can produce physical changes in the body such as interruptions in the menstrual cycle, temporary hair loss, and dizziness. Such changes may indicate more serious health complications. Report any such changes that you notice to your health care provider.

THE COMPLETE TRAVEL DIET complies with the United States government's Partnership for Healthy Weight Management, Voluntary Guidelines for Providers of Weight Loss Products or Services. This partnership is a coalition composed of representatives from science, academia, health care, government, commercial enterprises, and organizations promoting the public interest. More information about the coalition can be found on its Web site at www.consumer.gov/weightloss/guidelines.htm.

Using this guide

When you are traveling, be it on vacation or for business, your full attention is unlikely to be on losing weight—or should it be. Consequently, THE COMPLETE TRAVEL DIET is simple, straightforward, and easily followed. And although THE COMPLETE TRAVEL DIET was developed with an eye toward travelers, you don't have to be on a trip to follow its practical advice for weight loss and maintenance.

Note too that modifying your eating habits, your exercise routine, and your attitude will likely improve your overall physical and mental health. Your cholesterol level, your blood pressure, and your sleep patterns may all improve. These are all wonderful added benefits, but they are not the focus of THE COMPLETE TRAVEL DIET. That focus is simply to help you lose weight or maintain your body weight while you are "on the road."

TWO

Taking stock

Where you are

To create an effective plan for losing or maintaining your weight during your trip, you must first assess your current level of fitness, your Calorie needs, your dietary habits, and your attitudinal state. From these assessments you'll be able to establish a body weight goal and design a plan you can stick with to achieve that goal.

If you really want to know how you measure up healthwise, a thorough physical examination by a qualified physician

THE COMPLETE TRAVEL DIET

is the best way to go. It is the most reliable way to determine your current level of physical fitness as well as your ideal weight[1]. Indeed, you are encouraged to undergo a physical examination before making any drastic changes to your eating habits or activity levels.

On the other hand, the simple fact that you are reading this book is a pretty good indication that you would like to lose some weight, or at least maintain it while you are traveling. Whether it's the way you appear in the mirror, the way your clothes fit, or the numbers that you read off a scale, you already have a reasonable notion of where your weight is relative to where you'd like it to be.

Your fitness level

Although your sense of your body weight is probably a fairly reliable indicator of your physical condition, there are some "quick and dirty" measures of fitness that you may want to apply. These are much less rigorous than a physical exam but do provide a general idea of your level of fitness. For sure, there are as many measures of fitness as there are fitness "experts" to take those measurements. Measurements of physique are the most popular and typically use some form of gender-specific weight-to-height ratios. These measures are easy to calculate and do offer a rough measure of fitness.

---

[1] The notion of "ideal weight" is largely a personal matter. It is a weight where you feel attractive, fit, and content. Only you can determine your "ideal weight."

Body Mass Index

One of the most popular of these measures of stature is the Body Mass Index, or BMI. Your BMI is calculated by dividing your weight in kilograms by your height in meters squared, or

YOUR WEIGHT / (YOUR HEIGHT X YOUR HEIGHT)

Your BMI can also be calculated using English units. Multiply your weight in pounds by 705, then divide by your height in inches, then divide by your height in inches again, or:

((YOUR WEIGHT X 705) / YOUR HEIGHT) / YOUR HEIGHT

Or for an approximation of your BMI simply use the chart on the next page. The point at which your height intersects with your weight is your BMI.

An automatic BMI calculator is also available on THE COMPLETE TRAVEL DIET website at www.CompleteTravelDiet.com.

The U.S. National Heart, Lung, and Blood Institute has assigned the following designations to the listed ranges of BMI values:

BMI range	Fitness level
18.5 to 25	Healthy
25-29.9	Overweight
30 to 40	Obese
Greater than 40	Morbidly obese

Moreover, the Institute notes that if your BMI is greater than 25 and you have excess abdominal body fat, you are at especially high risk for obesity-related health problems. Specifically, if you are a man with a waist of more than 40 inches or a woman with a waist of 35 inches or greater, your risk of death is increased by up to 150 percent.

THE COMPLETE TRAVEL DIET

WEIGHT (pounds)	HEIGHT (feet, inches)					
	5'0"	5'3"	5'6"	5'9"	6'0"	6'3"
120	23	21	19	18	16	15
130	25	23	21	19	18	16
140	27	25	23	21	19	18
150	29	27	24	22	20	19
160	31	28	26	24	22	20
170	33	30	28	25	23	21
180	35	32	29	27	25	23
190	37	34	31	28	26	24
200	39	36	32	30	27	25
210	41	37	34	31	29	26
220	43	39	36	33	30	28
230	45	41	37	34	31	29
240	47	43	39	36	33	30
250	49	44	40	37	34	31

Body Mass Index

There are, however, exceptions. Some people who are deemed as "Overweight" can—and often are—more fit than their age and gender counterparts who fall well within the "Healthy" range. A body builder, for example, may have a BMI greater than 25 or even 30, but in this case a high BMI value reflects a high muscle mass rather than fat.

The BMI is not a perfect measurement of your health. There are many examples of healthy people of similar age, gender, height, and weight who are vastly different in the amount of body fat they carry. Certainly there are people with BMI measured values above 25 who are in better health than others whose BMI measured values fall well below 25. (Michael Jordan, at 6½ feet tall and 216 pounds, has a BMI of 25 and Arnold Schwarzenegger's BMI works out to be about 27. I doubt that anyone would say that these men are overweight—at least not to their faces.)

For the most part however, if you are in the "Overweight" category, even weight loss of as little as ten percent of body weight, if maintained over time, has been shown to be beneficial. Just remember to use the BMI as a guide, not as a bible.

Your Calorie needs

How many Calories do you need to consume each day to maintain your current weight? A rough—*very* rough—number of Calories an average person needs to consume in a day is 2000. But differences in height, weight, gender, age, and level of activity all affect one's Caloric needs. Obviously, the daily Calorie requirements to maintain the weight of a tall, active 230 pound man are quite different than those of a petite, sedentary 105 pound woman.

There are many factors involved in calculating how many Calories your body needs each day to maintain your current

THE COMPLETE TRAVEL DIET

weight. Most of these factors, however, can be captured by determining your basal metabolic rate and your physical activity.

Basal metabolic rate

Your basal metabolic rate is a measure of the Calories you need to function while at rest. This accounts for the majority of the Calories you burn each day to keep your body functioning—e.g., your lungs exchanging air, your heart pumping blood, your internal thermostat controlling your body's temperature, and your digestive tract breaking down the food you consume. Your basal metabolic rate can be calculated from a near century-old formula developed by J. Arthur Harris and Francis Benedict at Carnegie Institute of Washington in Boston.

Here are the basal metabolic rate (BMR) formulae for men and women:

BMR FOR MEN = 66 + (6.3 × BODY WEIGHT IN POUNDS) + (12.9 × HEIGHT IN INCHES) - (6.8 × AGE IN YEARS)

BMR FOR WOMEN = 655 + (4.3 × BODY WEIGHT IN POUNDS) + (4.7 × HEIGHT IN INCHES) - (4.7 × AGE IN YEARS)

Note: The Harris-Benedict formula does not take into account body mass. So while the formula holds for most people, extremely muscular people will need more Calories and obese people will need fewer.

Activity index

The other major factor in determining your Caloric needs to maintain your current body weight is your daily physical activity level. This includes every movement you make from retrieving your bags off an airport luggage carousel to running on a treadmill in a hotel gym. Select the descriptors below that best match the physical activity that you get while traveling; then use the number associated with that descriptor as a multiplier to the BMI value you calculated above.

TAKING STOCK

If you are **sedentary** (e.g., sit all day in transit then hit the snack bar) multiply your BMR by 1.2.

If you are **lightly active** (e.g., occasionally use the stairs instead of an escalator or do some light exercises a couple of times a week) multiply your BMR by 1.4.

If you are **moderately active** (e.g., walk to nearby destinations rather than using public transportation or do moderate exercises every other day) multiply your BMR by 1.5.

If you are **very active** (e.g., spend much of your day walking or exercise vigorously every other day) multiply your BMR by 1.6.

If you are **extremely active** (e.g., your day is filled with heavy lifting or you exercise hard almost every day) multiply your BMR by 1.8.

For example, the activity adjusted BMR for a 135 lb., 5 foot 5 inch, 38 year-old, moderately active woman, is 2044 Calories [1.5 × (655 + (4.3 × 135) + (4.7 × 65) - (4.7 × 38))].

For a 205 lb., 6 foot 2 inch, 58 year-old sedentary man, the activity adjusted BMR is 2301 Calories [1.2 × (66 + (6.3 × 205) + (12.9 × 74) - (6.8 × 58))].

THREE

Goals and plans

Where you want to be and how to get there

If you are reading this book, you probably have some weight goal in mind. And more than likely, that goal is to weigh less than you do now.

But is your weight goal realistic? Can you achieve it or at least begin to achieve it by the time you return home? And do you have a detailed plan in place to reach that goal?

Losing weight sensibly and safely while traveling can be a challenge. Continuing to lose weight and keeping that weight off once returning home can be an even greater challenge. These challenges require a plan to modify your eating habits

The Complete Travel Diet

and to add a reasonable amount of exercise to achieve a rational weight loss objective. If you are to be successful in maintaining or losing weight on your next trip, these elements are critical.

Goals

Without setting a realistic goal, your attempt to maintain your weight or to lose weight while traveling is unlikely to be successful. That is why, before you step out the door on your next trip, you need to set a weight goal for yourself that you hope to achieve by the time you return home. Though you may have in mind to ultimately lose a significant amount of weight over the coming weeks—and you can by following THE COMPLETE TRAVEL DIET—losing weight rapidly is unrealistic, unnecessary, and unlikely to be successful over the long haul.

Plan to lose weight gradually. Your weekly weight loss goal should be between one-half and two pounds per week. Anything less ambitious will tax your motivational skills. Anything greater can be unsafe and will probably be ineffective in the long run. Weight lost too rapidly on a trip will almost certainly return once you arrive back home.

Your weight goal at the conclusion of your trip should be based on your current body weight, not your ultimate weight goal. Specifically, your trip weight goal should be no more than a difference of one percent of your current weight per week of travel, but not more than two pounds [(YOUR CURRENT WEIGHT) − (YOUR CURRENT WEIGHT x 1% x WEEKS OF TRAVEL)].

For example if you weigh 150 pounds, your goal should be to weigh no less than 147 pounds after a two week trip. If you weigh 250 pounds, your goal should be nothing more ambitious than to shed the two pound limit during a one week trip.

If you are on an extended trip, adjust your diet and exercise routines periodically to continue to produce the recom-

GOALS AND PLANS

mended rate of weight loss of no more than one percent of your body weight per week (with a two pound limit).

A word of counsel: There is a good chance that you will come nowhere near your interim weight loss goal while you are traveling. Indeed, you may even gain weight. (Yikes!) This is especially true if you significantly increase the physical activity component of THE COMPLETE TRAVEL DIET because while you lose your stored fat you will be adding denser, heavier muscle fiber.

So it is important that you take the long view not only when setting weight loss goals but when measuring yourself against them. Measuring your progress on a daily basis can be discouraging. Your weight, as you lose, will not follow a smooth and consistent downward trend. Over a period of weeks and months, you will see changes, but on a daily basis your weight will occasionally increase. Losing weight is a long-term process and keeping it off is a life-time process.

Your attention while traveling should be focused less on weight loss and more on behavior change. Once eating patterns are changed and activity routines are established, the weight loss will follow even though it may not show up until weeks after you return from your trip. If you are committed to THE COMPLETE TRAVEL DIET, in the long run you can meet your goals.

Plans

Having a sensible goal in place is a necessary part of a weight control program. However, having realistic, specific, and livable plans to modify your diet, to increase your activity, and to inspire you to achieve that goal are even more important.

If you want to lose weight on your trip, you must reduce the average number of Calories you consume each day or increase your activity level, or—better yet—both. In the following pages, you will find advice to help you develop your own plan for eating, exercising, and keeping yourself motivated.

But don't expect that there will not be setbacks. There almost assuredly will be. Especially with all the variables that are out of your control when traveling, there will be times when you can't get in a planned activity or occasions when you eat too much of the wrong foods. I can almost guarantee that somewhere along the line, you will deviate from your plan.

Deviation from your plan, however, should not be cause for its abandonment. Instead, as you discover weaknesses in your plan, modify it to meet the circumstances of your travel. Just as you are in control of your body weight goal, you are in control of the plan to achieve it.

Behavioral plans

"I will lose three pounds on my next two-week trip," may be realistic and achievable during your next trip, but it is a goal, not a plan. To reach this or any other goal, you must make behavioral changes. Add to this goal a plan that, "I will eat no more than 1800 Calories a day and walk at least two miles every other day on my next two-week trip," and you'd have a plan with a behavioral basis.

Besides its focus on losing or maintaining weight while traveling, THE COMPLETE TRAVEL DIET sets itself apart from other programs in its concentration on behavior rather than weight loss. The notion here is that, short of medical intervention, changes in your body weight can only result from changes in your eating behaviors and your activity levels—things over which you have direct control. Those who are successful at losing weight and keeping that weight off concentrate on changing their eating and exercise habits, not on losing weight.

Genuine weight loss is a result of behavioral change, not the other way around. If you believe that you can starve your-

GOALS AND PLANS

self down to your weight goal and then change your eating and activity habits to keep you at that level, you will not succeed.

Realistic plans

Whatever weight you have gained over the past years was not likely added during a few days of travel. Likewise, it is unrealistic to expect that any behavioral changes that you adopt on your trip will be able to lead to a significant amount of weight loss, and your plan should reflect this reality. However, by using your travel time as an opportunity to make some small changes to your eating habits and activity levels, you will eventually lose the weight.

On the other hand, deciding to expand your exercise routine or restrict your diet while traveling may not be appropriate at all for your next trip. In such cases, you may want to postpone attempting to lose weight and strive instead at weight maintenance. For example, if you are on safari, it may be wise to limit your physical activities to those that would not take you beyond the protection of your camp. By the same token, if you are heading off for a tour touted as "The Great Restaurants of France," you would do well to simply maintain your weight. (If your tour is of "The Great Restaurants of Britain," that probably won't be a problem.)

Specific plans

- *"I will exercise more on my trip."*
- *"I will eat better while traveling."*
- *"I'll reduce the number of snacks I buy at airports."*

"More," "better," "reduce," and similar adverbs are all probably good concepts, but they are just that: Concepts. They are subjective and fuzzy and not a part of an effective weight loss plan, and because they can't be measured objectively, you will have no definite way of knowing if and when you are ful-

THE COMPLETE TRAVEL DIET

filling them or not. To reach your weight loss goal or sustain a maintenance level, the behavioral changes you plan to make must be specific and objective.

"I will walk to every appointment on my next sales trip," "I will eliminate eating butter while traveling," and "I will purchase only fresh fruit in airports from now on," are specific goals that can be objectively measured by anyone.

Livable plans

You can lose weight on almost any diet plan. However, to keep that weight off over time, you must be able to live with the requirements of that plan for the rest of your life. If you must struggle with a diet plan to make it fit into your life and travels, eventually you will abandon it.

Although there is no single "best" weight loss and maintenance plan, physicians and dietitians advise that programs which encourage slow, gradual weight loss are the healthiest, the easiest to follow, and the ones that are most likely to lead to permanent weight loss. THE COMPLETE TRAVEL DIET has been developed to be easily incorporated into your travel routines without interfering with your leisure or business activities. And it is easy to follow even after you return from your trip.

Losing a little weight while traveling doesn't require major changes in the way you normally travel. For instance, if you eat your morning slice of toast "dry" rather than with butter, you can eliminate around 100 Calories a day. Over a two week trip, that adds up to more than a one-third pound weight loss. If you add in a half-hour walk every day on your trip, you'll burn off another third of a pound or so.

Maybe that doesn't seem like much, but if you carry those habits back from your trip, you could lose in excess of 10 pounds over the course of a year just with these two easy-to-live-with changes.

GOALS AND PLANS

Follow through

It is not enough to simply put a plan in play. It must be monitored and reinforced.

Monitoring your progress

It's okay to step on the scale once, twice, or even more times a day. However, keep in mind that your weight will fluctuate naturally during the day and over the days. Moreover, when traveling, you would probably use different scales to measure your weight from day to day. Differences among scales are likely to be more dramatic than the natural fluctuation of your weight and certainly more than the fraction of a percent of your body weight that you are seeking. A better measurement of your progress will be how you feel and how your clothes fit.

If you are really interested in your weight change over the duration of your trip, take an average of one, four, and eight days prior to leaving and compare that to the average you get when weighing yourself one, four, and eight days after your return.

Rewarding your progress

Besides increased energy, better sleep, improved general health, and a more attractive appearance, some of the most significant rewards of losing excess weight are attitudinal: Knowing that you are in control of your health and fitness and appreciating that you can make changes for the better.

Nevertheless, under even the best of conditions, it can be difficult to abide by a plan you have set up for weight loss or maintenance. When you travel, staying the course can be even more difficult. So along the way you'll probably need other ways to reinforce your dieting and exercise behaviors.

THE COMPLETE TRAVEL DIET

Take every opportunity to reinforce your resolve. Provide incentives for yourself to keep your motivation up and to help you reach particular goals that you set for yourself—especially goals that are challenging. Choose rewards that you find personally important and/or desirable. Rewards may be shared with others, but they must be meaningful to you.

It should go without saying: Don't make food a reward. Instead, make a list of specific rewards that have a value to you and that are commensurate with the intermediate goals you are rewarding. For instance, for every five hours of recorded physical activity you log, rent a movie in your hotel room. For every 100 hours, shop for a new pair of sneakers. When you come in "on budget" seven days in a row in your daily food log, treat yourself to a massage. And as you are returning home after rigorously following your plan for weight loss or maintenance, treat yourself to a travel upgrade. Just keep in mind that interim successes are not measured by pounds but by behaviors.

FOUR

Nutrition

The basis of weight control

What your body needs to sustain your health while you are on the road and why it needs those components is a complex question, the answer to which is far from completely known. Indeed, researchers spend careers trying to understand the complexities of nutrition. Presented here is the basic, elementary version.

There are no differences in the nutritional requirements of travelers than there are for any other segment of the population. This chapter will cover how to fulfill those requirements while eliminating unneeded foods through eating a well-balanced, healthy diet.

THE COMPLETE TRAVEL DIET

The basic nutritional components you need to sustain your health while at the same time losing weight are carbohydrates, proteins, fats, fiber, vitamins, minerals, and water. Let's examine the role that each of these components plays in weight gain and, consequently, weight loss.

Carbohydrates

Carbohydrates provide fuel for your body. They are a necessary part of your diet and can help you to lose weight depending on the amount and source of the carbohydrates you choose to eat.

Carbohydrates come in two varieties: Simple and complex. During digestion, both types of carbohydrates break down into glucose, the primary source of energy for all your body's cells. Consequently it would seem that it shouldn't matter whether you receive your body's fuel from simple or complex carbohydrates. But it does matter. It matters a lot. So let's take a closer look at these types of fuel.

Simple carbohydrates

Simple carbohydrates are short, uncomplicated molecules—i.e., they are "simple." Because molecules of simple carbohydrates are small, they are readily absorbed in the intestines and delivered into the bloodstream without a need to be broken down any further. Simple carbohydrates can provide short-term increases in energy because they digest rapidly sending glucose into the bloodstream quickly.

Simple carbohydrates taste sweet and are the major component of refined sugar, the sort that is found in candies, cookies, donuts, processed crackers, sugary cereals, and soft drinks. Indeed, refined sugar is almost all simple carbohydrates.

NUTRITION

Simple carbohydrates are also found in fruits, which contain vitamins and minerals and are therefore more healthful than those that come from refined sugar. Moreover, because fruits also contain fiber, the absorption of fruit glucose (fructose) by your intestine is slowed and more evenly distributed over time. Without the slowing influence of fiber, simple carbohydrates enter the bloodstream immediately.

As the glucose is introduced into your bloodstream, this fuel has to go somewhere. If the muscles don't need it, it gets stored as body fat for future use. And if there is no future use? Well, it remains there (and there and there and there).

It is quite natural to have a "sweet tooth." Having an appetite for sweet things is normal and should not be denied. However, foods containing added sugars are typically low in nutrients and high in Calories. Consuming abundant quantities of sugary foods will prevent you from losing weight. If you want to lose weight, you must cut back on foods and drinks containing refined sugars. You can still satisfy your sweet tooth with fresh fruits.

Complex carbohydrates

Complex carbohydrates are also made up of sugars, but these sugar molecules are strung together to form longer, more complex chains. Unlike simple carbohydrates, complex carbohydrates are digested slowly so they provide a steadier source of energy. Complex carbohydrates are often referred to as starches and are found in rice, potatoes, pasta, whole grains, beans, and other legumes. Along with simple carbohydrates, they are also found in fresh fruits.

Beware, however, that processed or "refined" carbohydrates tend to act more like simple carbohydrates. They are quickly digested, causing more rapid fluctuations in your blood sugar. As a consequence, your hunger will be satisfied but is

The Complete Travel Diet

likely to return sooner than it would if you had eaten unprocessed carbohydrates.

Besides the fact that they provide for a more steady absorption of glucose by the intestine, the other nutritional advantages of eating foods rich in complex rather than simple carbohydrates is that they provide vitamins, minerals, and fiber.

About sixty percent of your Calories should be in the form of carbohydrates and most of those from complex carbohydrates.

Proteins

Carbohydrates provide your body's fuel. Protein, on the other hand, is essential in building, maintaining, and repairing your body's cellular structures. Protein is the major contributor to your body's defense against disease, and it also supports reproduction.

Protein is composed of materials called amino acids. Your body can manufacture many but not all amino acids that are necessary to maintain your health. The additional eight amino acids that are necessary for health must be consumed in your food. All types of foods contain protein but only foods from animal sources (e.g., meat, eggs, cheese) contain "complete" proteins that include the eight "essential" proteins that your body cannot manufacture.

Proteins also play an important part in weight loss. They have the effect of being able to immediately satiate you and they keep you feeling full for longer periods. They help you maintain muscle mass so that you are able to exercise to burn the Calories you consume. And when consumed with carbohydrates, they allow glucose to be absorbed more slowly and steadily, preventing insulin spikes that drain your energy and make you crave sugar.

NUTRITION

While it is important to include enough proteins in your daily diet to replenish these amino acids, it is likely that you consume too much rather than too little protein. About 10 percent of your daily Calories should come from protein—a little more if your exercise routine is more rigorous.

Fats

Dietary fats occur naturally in food. They are a concentrated source of energy for your body, they insulate your body tissues, and they help you feel full so you'll stop eating. They cannot be produced by your body so must be included in your diet.

Fats also play an important role in nutrition. They transport the fat-soluble vitamins A, D, E, and K and promote their absorption in your intestine. Fats are chemical compounds that contain fatty acids—molecules composed mostly of carbon and hydrogen atoms—and are the only source of the linoleic and linolenic acids, which are essential for cellular development and function.

Fats are important in your diet because they give food its taste, texture, consistency, stability, and palatability. They also play a role in food preparation by conducting heat during cooking, tenderizing the prepared food.

On the other hand, dietary fat gains the attention of weight reduction programs like THE COMPLETE TRAVEL DIET because on a per-weight basis, fats have more than twice as many Calories as carbohydrates or proteins. (Carbohydrates and proteins have about four Calories per gram while fats have about nine Calories per gram.)

Moreover, because dietary fats are more efficiently converted to body fat than are carbohydrates or proteins, excess dietary fat is more likely to be stored as body fat than either excess carbohydrates or proteins.

Depending on the chemical structure of these compounds, fats are, for the most part, parsed into saturated, monounsaturated, or polyunsaturated varieties.

Saturated fats

Fats that have the maximum possible number of hydrogen atoms attached to every carbon atom are said to be "saturated" with hydrogen atoms. Saturated fats are found mostly in foods of animal origin such as meat and dairy products. Some vegetable oils also contain saturated fat.

An easy way to recognize vegetable oils high in saturated fat is that they are usually solid at room temperature. Margarine, for instance, contains more saturated fat than does cooking oil. Both products still contain fat, however, and they both may have the same amount of Calories.

Saturated fats will tend to raise levels of Low Density Lipoproteins (LDL) cholesterol in your blood, a condition associated with heart disease.

Unsaturated fats

When the fatty acids composing a fat are missing hydrogen atoms, they are said to be "unsaturated." Unsaturated fats are found mostly in foods of plant origin and are also found in some seafoods.

Unsaturated fats—both monounsaturated and polyunsaturated—will reduce your blood cholesterol when they replace saturated fats in your diet. When possible, you should replace your consumption of saturated fat with unsaturated fat.

Monounsaturated fats

If unsaturated fats are missing one pair of atoms, they are called "monounsaturated." Monounsaturated fats are found primarily in vegetable oils from sources such as canola, olives, and peanuts. At room temperature monounsaturated fats are liquid. Unlike saturated fats, the consumption of monounsaturated fatty acids will tend to lower levels of LDL cholesterol in your blood.

Polyunsaturated fats

Like monounsaturated fats, polyunsaturated fats are liquid or soft at room temperature, and like monounsaturated fats their consumption will also tend to lower levels of LDL cholesterol in your blood. But unlike monounsaturated fats, their consumption will tend to lower the level of High Density Lipoprotein (HDL) cholesterol—the "good" cholesterol—in your blood.

Partially hydrogenated fats

Partial hydrogenation is a chemical process in which some of the missing hydrogen atoms of polyunsaturated fats are put back in. Partially hydrogenated fats take on "straighter" molecular structures which allow the molecules to pack more tightly together and thereby allow oils to solidify at higher temperatures. Vegetable shortening and margarine, for instance, are hydrogenated fats.

Partially hydrogenated fats act in much the same way as saturated fats in that they are high in Calories, can raise LDL cholesterol levels, and can also lower HDL cholesterol in the blood.

What fats to eat

No more than 30 percent of the Calories you consume each day should come from fat. If you are eating 2,000 Calories a day, this would be 65 grams of fat or fewer per day. Of those 65 grams, one-third should be from polyunsaturated fats (e.g., vegetable oils like safflower, corn, sunflower, and soybean) a little more than one-third from monounsaturated fats (e.g., extra-virgin olive oil, canola oil, pecans), and a little less than one-third from saturated and hydrogenated fats (e.g., tropical oils, fried foods, diary products, "marbled" meat, baked goods, processed foods).

Because fats are packed with Calories, their consumption can be a major contributor to excessive body weight. But it takes more than eating low-fat foods to lose weight and maintain that weigh loss.

Fiber

Technically, fiber is not a nutrient. It is just what it sounds like: A mass of slender, insoluble, threadlike structures of cells. Insoluble means that fiber is indigestible and passes through your body virtually intact so it provides no nutrition and no Calories. However, on its way through, it takes up space, giving a sensation of fullness so you are less likely to eat other, high-Calorie foods.

Fiber also plays other roles in weight loss. It interferes with the absorption of Calorie-dense dietary fat and it attaches to some proteins and fats that are consumed with it so that when it gets eliminated so too do those proteins and fats.

Fiber is found only in plant foods such as grains, vegetables, and fruits. These same fiber-rich food sources contain other nutritional components that have health benefits associated with them so that fiber, like most food components, is best obtained from the foods themselves rather than from supplements.

Vitamins

Vitamins facilitate the chemical reactions in your body that are necessary for good physical and mental health. Your body doesn't produce vitamins so they must come from your diet.

There are 13 vitamins that are essential to your body's functioning. They are vitamins A, C, D, E, K, and eight types of vitamin B. Vitamin C and all the B complex vitamins are water-soluble. That means that they aren't stored for long in your body. Consequently you must replace them daily.

The other vitamins (vitamins A, D, E, and K) are fat-soluble. These vitamins are easily stored by the body so you don't need to replace them frequently. In fact, consuming large amounts of these vitamins can easily become toxic.

Minerals

Many minerals are vital to the chemistry of your body to keep it functioning properly. In some cases, the body relies on large amounts of regularly consumed minerals. Calcium, potassium, and iron are such minerals. In other cases, such as the consumption of zinc, selenium, and copper, your body needs only relatively small amounts—i.e., "trace" amounts—to maintain good health.

Like vitamins, your body does not manufacture minerals. They must come from your diet.

Water

The most fundamental, the least sexy, and yet probably the most important component of a weight loss and maintenance program is water. Water has no food value—no vitamins,

THE COMPLETE TRAVEL DIET

no minerals, no Calories—but you can't survive without it. Water is the most plentiful substance in your body, but because your body can't store it, you must constantly keep it replenished.

FIVE

Diet

Body fuel

The foods that you eat and the fluids that you drink make up your diet. Over the last half century, however, "diet" has taken on another connotation. It has also come to mean controlling what we eat—primarily controlling what we eat so as to lose weight. (Aren't you reading this book in hopes of "going on a diet" to lose weight?)

Within this more limited definition of diet, how do you get the nutrition you need to keep yourself healthy while at the same time lose weight—all while you are traveling? The answer is simple: You manage what you eat and what you drink.

THE COMPLETE TRAVEL DIET

THE COMPLETE TRAVEL DIET provides you with the guidelines for that management.

Yes, you can lose weight by following diets that restrict portions to very small sizes or that exclude certain foods entirely. The problem is that these types of diets are generally not effective over the long run. They require unrealistic eating behaviors that cannot—and in many cases, should not—be continued over a long period. These "crash" diets can help you take off the pounds without encouraging the healthy lifestyle changes you need to maintain weight loss.

THE COMPLETE TRAVEL DIET is what is called in the diet industry—and it is a multi-billion dollar "industry" to be sure—an exchange-type diet. This type of diet not only is the most successful in helping people lose and keep off weight, it best fits the objective of THE COMPLETE TRAVEL DIET to be simple, adaptable, and flexible.

THE COMPLETE TRAVEL DIET recommends that you select a given number of servings from each of six food groups. Within each of those groups (and paying attention to portion sizes), you can choose whatever foods you desire. For example, in the complex carbohydrate category, you could choose either a slice of bread or half cup of oatmeal. Either food is counted as one serving.

Calories

A calorie is a measurement of energy. One calorie (as used by physicists) equals the amount of energy needed to raise (or lower) the temperature of one gram of water by one degree Celsius. This amount of energy is too small to describe the amount of energy in food so a dietary Calorie (with an uppercase "C") is used instead. A Calorie is 1000 (physics) calories, or the amount of energy to change the temperature of one liter of water one degree Celsius.

DIET

The more Calories a food has, the more energy it can provide to your body. When you eat more Calories than your body needs, it stores the extra Calories as fat. Hence, the principle of weight loss boils down to this: Eat as many Calories as your body consumes in energy and you will neither gain nor lose weight. Eat more Calories than you use and you will gain weight. Eat fewer Calories than your body burns and you will lose weight. Simple.

There is one caveat that accompanies this principle though. If you eat too few Calories, your body changes the rules. It will react to this apparent "starvation" by storing Calories more efficiently than it otherwise would. So while woman should, in general, try to limit their intake to no more than 1,500 Calories and men, in general, to fewer than 2,000 Calories, you should never eat fewer than 1,000 Calories per day. And if your level of physical activity increases significantly during your travels, you may need to *increase* your Calorie intake (especially protein Calories) as you replace body fat with muscle.

Of the seven dietary components described in the previous chapter, only carbohydrates, proteins, and fats provide Calories. Fiber, vitamins, minerals, and water, while necessary, contain no energy producing Calories. By following a well-balanced, reduced-Calorie diet of carbohydrates, proteins, and fats, you will lose weight while maintaining your health. And just as importantly, if not more importantly, you will be able to keep the weight off.

The one pound rule

The mathematics of Calorie storage and use is simple. If you consume 3,500 Calories more than your body uses, those Calories will be stored as about one pound of body fat. On the other hand, if your body burns 3,500 Calories more than you consume, your weight will decrease by about one pound.

THE COMPLETE TRAVEL DIET

You can see how eliminating just 100 Calories a day can, over time, make a significant difference in your body weight. By cutting out snacks, sodas, and other sugary foods from your diet and/or exercising just another 20 minutes a day, you will lose weight. It is as simple as that.

Counting Calories

It is difficult enough to keep track of the Calories you consume and burn while you are at home. Traveling–eating in different restaurants every day and varying the exercise you get–can be even more challenging. That is why THE COMPLETE TRAVEL DIET uses the Food Guide Pyramid as its standard. Instead of having to calculate the Caloric content of food sources, you only have to keep track of a handful of food groups and the number of servings from each you should consume.

Being an exchange-type diet, THE COMPLETE TRAVEL DIET allows for a wide variety of foods and is relatively easy to follow when away from home. More importantly, however, is that THE COMPLETE TRAVEL DIET will get you used to making wise food selections which are necessary to continue to lose weight and to keep it off after returning home.

Food Guide Pyramid

Your diet—whether you are trying to lose weight, maintain your weight, or even gain weight—should be composed of a variety of low-Calorie, nutrient-rich foods. One way to get that variety is to follow the guidelines of the Food Guide Pyramid shown on page 42.

The Food Guide Pyramid was developed by the United States Department of Agriculture (USDA) and the Department of Health and Human Services as a general guide to choosing a healthful assortment of foods. And while the idea of a weight loss diet is to consume fewer Calories, the variety of foods from

DIET

which those Calories come should be in the same proportions as recommended by the Food Guide Pyramid.

The Food Guide Pyramid consists of the "five basic food groups" of (1) bread, cereal, pasta, and rice; (2) vegetables; (3) fruits; (4) milk, yogurt and cheese; and (5) meat, poultry, fish, dry beans, eggs, and nuts. A sixth group (fats, oils, and sweets) consists of non-essential items that are tasty but are also high in fat and/or Calories and should be eaten, if at all, in moderation.

Each block of the pyramid represents a different food group. The size of the block more or less corresponds to the number of recommended servings: The larger the block, the greater the number of servings of that particular food group.

> **NOTICE**
>
> The Food Guide Pyramid was last updated in 1992. There is currently a recommendation from the White House Office of Management and Budget to revise the Food Guide Pyramid to take into account the increased risks of heart disease due to trans fatty acids and the lowering of risks of heart disease from omega-3 fatty acids in the diet. A revision to the food guide pyramid may come as early as 2005.

At the base of the pyramid is the starch block, which is comprised of carbohydrate-rich foods. Most of the food you eat every day should come from this largest pyramid block.

The next tier up on the pyramid includes the vegetable and fruit blocks. Foods in these blocks are good sources of vitamins, minerals, and fiber and should make up a significant portion of your daily diet.

Above the vegetable and fruit groups are the food blocks containing protein from animal and vegetable sources.

THE COMPLETE TRAVEL DIET

Finally, sitting atop the pyramid is the smallest block containing fats, oils, and sweets. Foods in this block should be used sparingly.

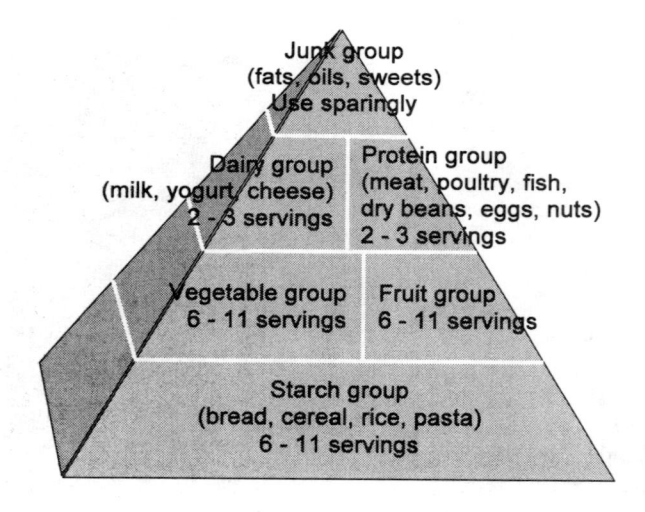

```
                    Junk group
                  (fats, oils, sweets)
                    Use sparingly

         Dairy group        Protein group
    (milk, yogurt, cheese)  (meat, poultry, fish,
       2 - 3 servings       dry beans, eggs, nuts)
                              2 - 3 servings

      Vegetable group        Fruit group
       6 - 11 servings      6 - 11 servings

              Starch group
       (bread, cereal, rice, pasta)
            6 - 11 servings
```

Food Guide Pyramid*

*The names of the food item groups have been modified for THE COMPLETE TRAVEL DIET

As you may have noticed, many foods overlap Food Guide Pyramid designations. For example, citrus fruits also contain a good portion of carbohydrates. As a general rule, you should assign food items to their predominant block on the Food Guide Pyramid but at the same time be aware that they can contribute to unfulfilled servings in other blocks.

DIET

Adherence to the relative proportions of the foods groups recommended by the Food Guide Pyramid has been questioned by diet gurus who suggest alternative strategies to weight reduction. The Food Guide Pyramid, however, is based on current research findings and is at the foundation of THE COMPLETE TRAVEL DIET. By following an eating plan that includes the proportion of foods in the Food Guide Pyramid, you will be assured of getting all the essential nutrients you need for good health while you are traveling.

Starch group (bread, cereal, rice, pasta)

As you can see in the Food Guide Pyramid, the foundation of a nutritious diet begins with grain products—bread, cereal, rice, and pasta. Most of the Calories in your diet should come from this group—the single largest food group in the Food Guide Pyramid.

These "grain foods" provide complex carbohydrates for energy and are generally low in fat. They become high-fat foods when you add sauces, oils, or other high-fat toppings like butter, sour cream, or mayonnaise.

"Whole grain" foods in particular supply vitamins, minerals, dietary fiber, and other plant compounds called phytochemicals. Milling or "refining" removes the bran (the outer, fiber-rich layer of the grain) and the germ (the inner, nutrient-rich portion of grains). Look for meals prepared with whole or cracked wheat, whole barley, whole oats, graham flour, whole cornmeal, rye, or brown rice.

If you are like most people who struggle to control your weight, you are probably consuming only one serving of whole grains a day—perhaps even less. Worse yet, on the road whole grain foods are more difficult to come by while processed grains can be found in a large variety of food sources. You may have to go a little out of your way or make an extra effort to incorporate whole grain foods into your diet while traveling.

THE COMPLETE TRAVEL DIET

By eating even the minimum number of servings recommended by the Food Guide Pyramid, you will consume at least 100 grams of carbohydrates per day. This is necessary to prevent fatigue and dangerous fluid imbalances.

Vegetable group

Most vegetables are naturally low in fat and Calories and many are high in fiber. The Food Guide Pyramid recommends three to five servings of vegetables each day. Choose whole vegetables over vegetable juice. When you consume the skin and membranes of vegetables you get every bit of fiber they contain, so when possible, avoid peeling them. This will require that they be washed (not just soaked) in warm water to remove any dirt and bacteria that may be on the skin.

> ### Packaged produce
>
> When vegetables and fruits are harvested, they begin to lose their nutrients. Without being chilled or preserved, nearly half of the vitamins in produce may be lost within a few days. If refrigerated, this loss may be postponed to a week or two. So produce that has been properly handled and quickly processed by freezing or canning can be even more nutritious than fresh produce sold in stores.
>
> On the other hand, the heating that takes place in the canning process can wipe out up to a half of the content of vitamin A, vitamin C, riboflavin, and thiamin. And for every year in storage, an additional 5 to 20 percent of these vitamins are lost.

Starchy vegetables such as white potatoes, sweet potatoes or corn, can be counted as servings in the vegetable group or in the starch food group, but not both. Similarly, dry beans, peas, and lentils can be counted as servings in the vegetable group or in the protein group, but not both.

Fruit group

When possible choose whole fruit over fruit juice. Juices often have added sugar and like vegetables, eating the skin and membranes of fruit ensures that you get every bit of fiber. (Be sure to wash the skins thoroughly before the fruits are eaten.)

Dairy group (milk, yogurt, cheese)

Dairy products are a good source of protein, which helps build muscles and keeps organs working properly. They also contain calcium, which keeps bones strong and healthy, and vitamin D to help process the calcium that is ingested.

The caveat for this food group is that many of the foods have a high fat content. Fortunately, many low-fat and fat-free products can be found here. These dairy products are as nutritious as whole milk food products they replace, but they are lower in fat and Calories. Whenever possible, choose skim or low-fat milk, fat-free or low-fat yogurt, low-fat cheese, and reduced-fat ice cream over their "full-fat" alternatives.

And if you are sensitive to some dairy foods or if you are lactose intolerant (i.e., can't digest a type of sugar found in milk and other dairy products), you can often find lactose-free dairy products that are low-fat or fat-free.

Protein group (meat, poultry, fish, dry beans, eggs, nuts)

While many foods include protein, the foods that populate this group are called "proteins" because they are more heavily packed with proteins than foods that are generally found in the other food groups of the Food Guide Pyramid.

Meat and poultry contain saturated fat and cholesterol but are good sources of protein and nutrients such as iron and zinc that are important for your health. Fish is lower in saturated fat and cholesterol than meat or poultry and also contains protein and other nutrients. Most beans and bean products are rich sources of protein, are high in fiber, and are almost fat-free.

THE COMPLETE TRAVEL DIET

Beans such as pinto, navy, kidney, and black beans can also count as servings of vegetables

Nuts are a good source of protein, though they are high in Calories and fat. On the other hand, they are generally low in saturated fat and have no cholesterol. Choose raw rather than boiled, sautéed, or, of course, nuts coated with sugar.

Junk group (fats, oils, sweets)

On first blush, it would seem only reasonable that if you wanted to lose "fat," you should drastically limit your intake of foods high in "fat." Unfortunately, it's not that simple. Reducing dietary fat without reducing Calories will not lead to weight loss.

Though they share the same name, body fat and dietary fat are different things. Dietary fat—the kind that is found in the foods that you consume—is different than body fat—the kind that is stored in your body and hangs over your underwear. Nevertheless, you are right to make the connection between the two, for fats contain about twice the number of Calories than do equal amounts of carbohydrates or proteins.

Similarly, oils like those used in fast-food preparation are often fats in liquid form, and sweets are..., well, sweet because of relatively large measures of processed sugar used in the recipes for these food items. So a great way to cut back on Calories is to reduce your intake of fats, oils, and sweets.

Junk replacements

The junk food group contains the tastiest foods in the Food Guide Pyramid. They are also the least nutritious and the most Calorie-dense. Consequently, food processing companies have been active in seeking to find replacements for the high-Calorie constituents in these foods.

DIET

Fat replacers

Fat replacers reduce a food's fat content while attempting to maintain the pleasing characteristics that fat contributes to the food such as texture and flavor. For the most part, however, fat replacers have found limited application. They don't seem to be a good enough match for the sensory qualities that fat adds to food, and some fat replacers have undesirable side-effects such as the production of gas.

Of greater concern to dieters is that extra sugars are sometimes added to make up for the deficit in taste and texture that is caused by the removal of fat. Indeed, some fat-free foods have even more Calories than their "regular" counterparts. This can be a double whammy for you if you are among the people who have a tendency to eat more of a food that is labeled "low-fat," "reduced-fat," or "fat-free."

Still there may be value in using fat replacers in your diet if you understand that low-fat and fat-free foods are not necessarily low-Calorie or Calorie-free foods. Extra Calories, whether from regular, low-fat, or fat-free foods, all get stored as body fat.

Sugar substitutes

If you just can't get along without sugar in your coffee—you really can, you know—or a cookie now and then, consider using a sugar substitute. Sugar substitutes offer the taste of sweetness without significant Calories. Foods containing sugar substitutes such as sorbitol, saccharin, and aspartame, however, may not

> **Healthful sugars?**
>
> By the way, brown or "raw" sugar is no more healthful than plain old sugar. It is nothing more than refined white sugar with a touch of molasses, which provides only an insignificant trace of nutrients. Honey, too, has only trace amounts of nutrients.

47

necessarily be lower in Calories than similar products that contain sugar. Simply because a food contains a substitute instead of the real thing doesn't necessarily make it lower in Calories than a similar product that contains sugar. And of course, adding an artificial sweetener to a food cannot reduce the Calories in that food.

Moreover, artificial sweeteners are not always effective in satisfying a craving for sweets or carbohydrates. In fact, their frequent use may get you accustomed to the sweet taste so that you desire more of that taste rather than less.

Fiber

In addition to the foods of the Food Guide Pyramid, the consumption of fiber plays an important role in weight loss and maintenance. Fiber contributes to the efficient operation of your digestive system and can help you feel full without the contribution of any Calories.

A daily fiber intake of 20 to 30 grams will help in proper bowel function. If you eat the recommended number of servings of fruits, vegetables, and grain foods, suggested by the Food Guide Pyramid, you should have no trouble getting 25 to 30 grams of fiber a day.

Breakfast is perhaps the best time to enjoy fiber-rich foods because fiber is plentiful in grains. Oatmeal, bran cereals, and whole-bran muffins or waffles supply about one-quarter of your daily fiber needs. When topped with fruit, that figure can go up to one-half.

Good options for the rest of the day are vegetables and fruits and remember that the skins of vegetables and fruits are where the fiber is really concentrated.

DIET

Beverages

Although they aren't on the Food Guide Pyramid, don't overlook what you drink as well as what you eat. Coffee, tea, sodas, fruit drinks, or alcoholic beverages, are often consumed between meals or are imbibed with food to enhance the enjoyment of those meals. But...

Coffee and Tea

A natural constituent of coffee and tea is caffeine. Many convenience drinks and some food products also contain caffeine. When consumed in sensible quantities, caffeine is a safe way to stay alert. It is a stimulant that begins its effect about 15 minutes after consumption and peaks in effect in about an hour. But caffeine can also trigger a drop in blood sugar, increasing the chance of a sugar craving.

Coffee and tea are fairly low in Calories and may be good alternatives to sweetened drinks, but the Calorie count of these beverages jumps when sugar or whiteners are added.

Foods prepared with coffee (e.g., ice cream and frozen yogurt) can also contain significant amounts of caffeine and can be loaded with sugar. And coffee drinks can make up nearly a third(!) of your daily Calorie allotment.

Convenience drinks

Besides possibly containing caffeine, sodas and fruit-based sugar drinks are typically high in Calories while supplying few or no nutrients. For example a 12-ounce can of cola has 150 Calories, and a 20-ounce bottle of Sunkist® Orange Soda contains no juice but 325 Calories.

Alcohol

Alcohol is high in Calories—very high. A glass of wine can contain 100 Calories. What's more, when ingested in suffi-

THE COMPLETE TRAVEL DIET

cient quantities, it interferes with rational thought and can lower your resolve.

Water

Water accounts for over half your body weight and plays important roles in weight loss and maintenance. For instance your kidneys rely on water to eliminate waste from your body. When you don't drink enough water, the liver steps in to help your kidneys flush out that waste. As a consequence, your liver becomes less efficient at its role in converting stored fat for use as energy—a very important role indeed when you are cutting back on Calories. Drinking plenty of water ensures that your kidneys will be able to do their job and your liver its.

Water also acts as an appetite suppressant. The signals from your stomach that tell your brain that it is full don't include messages indicating the nature of the contents that have filled it. Drinking water throughout the day to keep your stomach full can trick your body into thinking it is satisfied.

The problem with water, though—especially when you are traveling—is that your body can't store it. You must constantly replenish it. Try to drink at least eight to ten, 8-ounce glasses of water or water-based beverages per day. (If you will be more active during your travels, increase that amount.) You can also get water through the consumption of vegetables, fruits, and dairy products because large portions of those foods are water.

Servings and portions

How much you eat is as much a factor in weight control as is what you eat. In fact, controlling the amount you eat can be much more of a challenge to a dieter, especially a traveler, than food selection. And making it even more challenging can

DIET

be a lack of understanding of the difference between a "serving" and a "portion."

Servings

Depending on your stature and activity level, the Food Guide Pyramid recommends eating a certain number of servings—not a certain number of Calories—of foods from each of the food groups. The lower numbers of servings in the ranges shown are for people such as sedentary women and some older adults who should consume about 1,600 Calories a day. The higher numbers of servings in the ranges are for people such as teenage boys, active men, and very active women, who should consume about 2,800 Calories a day. The recommended servings for most of us will fall somewhere in between these extremes.

With a few exceptions, one serving of any of the foods in a particular food group has about the same number of Calories

Food Group	Calories per serving
Starch	80
Vegetable	25
Fruit	60
Dairy group (whole fat)	150
Dairy group (fat-free)	80
Protein (fatty meats)	225
Protein (medium fat meats)	165
Protein (lean meats)	75
Junk	50

Approximate Calories per serving for foods in each of the food groups

THE COMPLETE TRAVEL DIET

as a serving of any other food in that group. A table of the approximate Caloric content for each of the food groups of the Food Guide Pyramid is shown on the previous page. Notice that two of the foods groups (dairy and protein) are further divided because for these particular food groups, Caloric content varies dramatically depending on the fat content of the food item.

There is variance in this generality, but for the purposes of THE COMPLETE TRAVEL DIET, the Caloric content of a single serving of any food in each of the nine food categories listed on page 51 is treated the same.

If you are seeking to maintain your weight while you travel, plan your number of daily servings accordingly. If, for example, you are traveling overseas to your destination and you will be sedentary for much of the day, you should lean toward consuming a smaller number of servings. If you plan to be active—for instance, you will be hiking much of the time—you can increase the number of servings to the higher range. On the other hand, if you plan to lose, rather than to simply maintain your weight, cut back on the number of servings but keep the proportions among the food groups the same.

It is ideal to satisfy the recommended servings of the Food Guide Pyramid every day, but it can be difficult to eat foods in the same proportions as suggested, especially while traveling. Not helping in this matter is the fact that most portions served up in restaurants are larger—often very much larger—than the serving sizes recommended by the Food Guide Pyramid.

Nevertheless, try to eat no more than two to three servings from any food group during any one meal, and spread your meals throughout the day. If you find that your food selections are skewed on one day, try to balance out for the disproportion on the following day or two so that your daily average works out to be in line with the recommendations.

Serving sizes

Serving size depends on the particular food in question. The only accurate way to determine the size of a serving of a particular food is to weigh it—not so practical when traveling. So, for THE COMPLETE TRAVEL DIET to be useful, such accuracy is sacrificed in favor of simplicity and convenience.

To help give you a sense of serving sizes, here are some samples from each of the food groups of the Food Guide Pyramid.

Starch group

In the starch group, one serving is any one of the following: A slice of whole-grain bread, a tortilla, a half of a hamburger bun, a half of an English muffin, a half of a bagel, a small pancake, a small waffle, ¼ cup low-fat granola, ½ cup (an ice cream scoop-sized amount) of cooked cereal or rice or pasta or mashed potatoes, 3 cups of popped popcorn (without the butter, of course), or three to four crackers.

Vegetable group

As a general rule, a serving size of vegetables is about ½ cup for cooked vegetables or vegetable juice, and about 1 cup for raw vegetables. For convenience, think of one serving of vegetables as being about the size of your fist, or the amount that would fill the volume of a tennis ball or a baseball—a little more if the vegetables are loosely packed like salad fixings, a little less if the vegetables are more tightly packed like chopped or cooked vegetables or like a baked potato.

Fruit group

Like the vegetable group, a serving size is about ½ cup if the fruit is chopped, cooked, or canned—again about the size of

THE COMPLETE TRAVEL DIET

a tennis ball or baseball. One serving of dried fruit, because the water has been removed, is about the same size as a golf ball.

Whole, roundish, medium-sized fruits such as apples, oranges, peaches, and pears are one serving each. A half of larger roundish fruits such as grapefruits, papayas, mangoes, and melons are about one serving each. A banana is about one serving. Two plums are a serving as are four apricots.

Dairy group

One cup of milk or yogurt is about one serving. That's about a medium-sized glass. Likewise, one scoop of ice cream or ice milk is about one serving.

Serving sizes for cheeses are much smaller: Only about 1½ ounces of natural cheese or 2 ounces of processed cheese is a serving. That's about the size of a pair of dice or the size of your thumb.

Protein group

One serving from the protein food group is about 3 ounces. That is about the amount of meat, poultry, or fish that is served on a sandwich. It is also about a half of a chicken breast, a small hamburger, a small fish filet, or an egg.

Junk group

As you might guess, here at the top of the Food Guide Pyramid, serving sizes are downright miniscule. Indeed, serving sizes for many of the items in the junk food group are so small that they are referred to as "bits" or "dashes." For instance, a serving of a snack food such as pretzels or chips is about the size of a golf ball. A fortune cookie, half of a macaroon, or four gumdrops is one serving.

There is no need to abandon eating the foods in this group, but as you can see, you must do so sparingly.

Serving sizes simplified

Because foods come in all sorts of sizes and shapes, "serving size" can be a little overwhelming. Fortunately, servings usually are what they appear. For example, a medium size apple is one serving from the fruit group, an egg is one serving from the protein group, a slice of bread is one serving from the starch group, a glass of milk is one serving from the dairy group, and a caramel is one serving from the junk group. It can get a little tricky when, for instance, you are trying to figure out how to portion out a slice of pizza, but for purposes of THE COMPLETE TRAVEL DIET and its principle to keep it simple, let your intuition be your guide.

If you really want to know what a serving looks like, the next time you prepare your own meal at home, measure out exact serving sizes, and put them on a plate or in a glass so you can calibrate your perception of serving size (e.g., a cup of milk, two ounces of processed cheese, three ounces of lean steak, or a tablespoon of sugar). And if you really, *really* want to be precise, you can check some of the dietary sources listed in the Resources chapter or tap into the USDA's National Nutrient Database at www.CompleteTravelDiet.com.

The food ball

Even with a keen sense of serving size, however, it is difficult to determine exact serving sizes when eating your meals on the road. The sizes of plates, cups, and glasses in which meals are served and the presentation style of those meals all factor into your perception of serving size. So, keeping with the theme of THE COMPLETE TRAVEL DIET of simplicity over accuracy, use this rule of thumb: Except for the junk food group (which you should be avoiding anyway) and cheeses from the dairy food group, a serving is roughly what you can hold in the palm of your hand or the volume of a baseball or a tennis ball or the "food ball" shown on the next page. A small piece of fruit, a

THE COMPLETE TRAVEL DIET

small chicken breast, a small steak, a small potato are examples of single servings.

The food ball
Approximate size of one serving from the starch, vegetable, fruit, dairy, or protein food groups

The food stack

While the food ball is a simple way to size up servings of food items that you can picture holding in your hand, much of what is delivered on your plate is unlikely to come in the shape

DIET

The food stack
Approximate size of one serving from the starch, vegetable, fruit, dairy, or protein food groups

of a ball. So here is a corresponding rule of thumb: Again, except for the junk food group and cheeses, a serving is roughly the size of the "food stack" represented above. A serving of oatmeal or rice or berries or yogurt are examples of single servings that are the size of the food stack.

The junk food ball

The USDA provides no specific serving size for the junk food group because you should eat foods from this group only "sparingly." Nevertheless, to provide some guidance, the ball shown on the next page will give you a rough idea—a very rough idea—of the serving size of an item from the junk food group as well as cheeses from the dairy food group.

For sugar-based foods such as candy and for the cheeses from the dairy food group, the junk food ball is a little larger. For fat-packed foods like chips, it's a little smaller. But if you stick to serving sizes for junk foods and for cheeses that are about the size of the junk food ball, you should be within reasonable serving size measures.

The junk food ball
Approximate size of one serving
from the junk food group

Portions

Simply put, a "serving" is a food specific, standard unit of measure as determined by the USDA for use with the Food Guide Pyramid (e.g., a slice of bread, a medium-sized apple, an egg). A "portion," on the other hand, is the amount of food on your plate. A plate-full of pasta is one portion, but it may be three or four servings. A 12-ounce steak can be one portion, but it is four servings. You get the idea. It isn't a difficult distinction.

Very often, however, these terms are intermixed. When a menu promises to deliver a "single serving," of a food item, you can only be sure that you will receive a "single portion." That portion could easily be two, three, or even more "servings" as defined by the Food Guide Pyramid and used in THE COMPLETE TRAVEL DIET.

Terms

Low-fat. Fat-free. Reduced-Calorie. What the heck do all these terms mean?

The United States Food and Drug Administration (FDA) has set up regulations for specific dietary terms used to label food products. The same guidelines apply to restaurant menu items as well. If you are traveling in the United States, you can have some assurance that the terms have consistent meanings though differences in suppliers, recipes, and chefs can easily change an item shown on a menu as "low-fat" to a food delivered to your table that is nowhere near low-fat.

The following definitions of terms are presented here verbatim from the FDA's regulations.

> The regulations spell out what terms may be used to describe the level of a nutrient in a food and how they can be used. These are the core terms:
>
> **Free.** This term means that a product contains no amount of, or only trivial or "physiologically inconsequential" amounts of, one or more of these components: fat, saturated fat, cholesterol, sodium, sugars, and calories. For example, "calorie-free" means fewer than 5 calories per serving, and "sugar-free" and "fat-free" both mean less than 0.5 g per serving. Synonyms for "free" include "without," "no" and "zero." A synonym for fat-free milk is "skim".
>
> **Low.** This term can be used on foods that can be eaten frequently without exceeding dietary guidelines for one or more of these components: fat, saturated fat, cholesterol, sodium, and calories. Thus, descriptors are defined as follows:

Low-fat: 3 g or less per serving.
Low-saturated fat: 1 g or less per serving.
Low-sodium: 140 mg or less per serving.
Very low sodium: 35 mg or less per serving.
Low-cholesterol: 20 mg or less and 2 g or less of saturated fat per serving.
Low-calorie: 40 calories or less per serving.

Synonyms for low include "little," "few," "low source of," and "contains a small amount of."

Lean and extra lean. These terms can be used to describe the fat content of meat, poultry, seafood, and game meats.

Lean: less than 10 g fat, 4.5 g or less saturated fat, and less than 95 mg cholesterol per serving and per 100 g.

Extra lean: less than 5 g fat, less than 2 g saturated fat, and less than 95 mg cholesterol per serving and per 100 g.

High. This term can be used if the food contains 20 percent or more of the Daily Value for a particular nutrient in a serving.

Good source. This term means that one serving of a food contains 10 to 19 percent of the Daily Value for a particular nutrient.

Reduced. This term means that a nutritionally altered product contains at least 25 percent less of a nutrient or of calories than the regular, or reference, product. However, a reduced claim can't be made on a product if its reference food already meets the requirement for a "low" claim.

DIET

Less. This term means that a food, whether altered or not, contains 25 percent less of a nutrient or of calories than the reference food. For example, pretzels that have 25 percent less fat than potato chips could carry a "less" claim. "Fewer" is an acceptable synonym.

Light. This descriptor can mean two things:

> First, that a nutritionally altered product contains one-third fewer calories or half the fat of the reference food. If the food derives 50 percent or more of its calories from fat, the reduction must be 50 percent of the fat.

> Second, that the sodium content of a low-calorie, low-fat food has been reduced by 50 percent. In addition, "light in sodium" may be used on food in which the sodium content has been reduced by at least 50 percent.

> The term "light" still can be used to describe such properties as texture and color, as long as the label explains the intent—for example, "light brown sugar" and "light and fluffy."

Healthy. A "healthy" food must be low in fat and saturated fat and contain limited amounts of cholesterol and sodium. In addition, if it's a single-item food, it must provide at least 10 percent of one or more of vitamins A or C, iron, calcium, protein, or fiber. Exempt from this "10-percent" rule are certain raw, canned and frozen fruits and vegetables and certain cereal-grain products. These foods can be labeled "healthy," if they do not contain ingredients that change the nutritional profile, and, in the case of enriched grain products, conform to standards of identity, which call for certain required ingredients.

If it's a meal-type product, such as frozen entrees and multi-course frozen dinners, it must provide 10 percent of two or three of these vitamins or minerals or of protein or fiber, in addition to meeting the other criteria. The sodium content cannot exceed 360 mg per serving for individual foods and 480 mg per serving for meal-type products.

Percent fat free: A product bearing this claim must be a low-fat or a fat-free product. In addition, the claim must accurately reflect the amount of fat present in 100 g of the food. Thus, if a food contains 2.5 g fat per 50 g, the claim must be "95 percent fat free."

Meals and main dishes: Claims that a meal or main dish is "free" of a nutrient, such as sodium or cholesterol, must meet the same requirements as those for individual foods. Other claims can be used under special circumstances. For example, "low-calorie" means the meal or main dish contains 120 calories or less per 100 g. "Low-sodium" means the food has 140 mg or less per 100 g. "Low-cholesterol" means the food contains 20 mg cholesterol or less per 100 g and no more than 2 g saturated fat. "Light" means the meal or main dish is low-fat or low-calorie.

Meal replacements

Meal replacement drinks and shakes can be the perfect companion for travelers. They can provide adequate nutrients while controlling Calories. Meal replacements are handy but cannot take the place of whole foods for an extended period.

The real advantage that meal replacement drinks and shakes have for the traveler is, not so much that they replace whole-food meals but that they replace less healthy meals that travelers tend to "grab" between flights, in rest areas, or while otherwise on the road. Indeed meal replacements can not only save you from consuming less healthy foods, they can also save you time and money.

Supplements

If your daily Calorie intake target is less than 1,200 Calories, you should consider taking a daily vitamin and mineral supplement to make sure you get all the nutrients you need. Just keep in mind that supplements are just that: Supplements. They should fill in nutritional gaps that can open in your diet while traveling and are not substitutes for eating nutrient-rich foods.

When selecting dietary supplements, you can generally disregard claims for "natural" or "herbal" products. Those that claim to be natural or herbal are not usually tested scientifically to prove that they are more potent or more effective than synthetic supplements or that they are even safe.

Snacks

By maintaining a relatively steady blood sugar level over the course of the day, you will avoid spells of hunger and food cravings. This means eating every three to four hours and is where snacks come in to play.

Snacks are simply smaller meals that can, over the course of a day, make up a significant portion of your daily Caloric intake. In and of themselves, snacks are not necessarily any less healthful than regular meals. Instead it is the kind of food that you choose as a snack that can pack on the Calories.

Select foods for your snacks with the same care you do for your regular meals of breakfast, lunch, and dinner and you will find that you will be satisfied and still remain within your

THE COMPLETE TRAVEL DIET

daily Calorie budget. And if you do opt for "snack foods," just be sure to select low-fat varieties.

Medications

Some medications can interfere with weight loss. Drugs prescribed for asthma, arthritis, depression, diabetes, inflammatory bowel disease, lupus, and birth control can hamper weight maintenance or loss. Some may even cause weight gain. If you are taking prescription medications for these or other conditions, consult with your physician to learn if there are alternative medications that will not impede your efforts to maintain or lose weight while traveling.

Eating habits

Major principles of a healthy diet on which you can maintain or lose weight are ones of dietary variety, moderation, and balance.

Variety

If you eat the proportionate servings recommended by the Food Guide Pyramid over the course of a day, you will get the nutrients you need from varied sources in moderate portion sizes. Moreover, by choosing a variety of foods from within each of the basic food groups of the Food Guide Pyramid, you will get a good mix of soluble and insoluble fiber, and you will be able to control the Calories you take in to maintain or lose weight.

If you are traveling, variety in your diet is something that should come easily. Traveling is an opportunity to try new foods and new ways in which familiar foods are prepared. Indeed, variety of food sources can be one of the more rewarding parts of travel.

Moderation

When "going on a diet," you may tend to concentrate on not eating too much. But there is another concern: Eating too little. If you cut back on your daily Caloric intake by more than about 500 Calories, you may not get all the nutrients you need. You may find yourself with less energy rather than less weight because you will be sending a message to your body that food is getting scarce. In turn, your body will attempt to store whatever it can to prepare for that deprivation.

Sleep

There is evidence that not getting a good night's sleep can interfere with your body's ability to process glucose. Sleep deprivation may leave you feeling less satiated and encourage your body to stockpile Calories. The result: a craving for carbohydrates and sweets, which in turn get stored as fat.

Balance

A program of weight maintenance or loss, especially a program for travelers, has to advocate eating a balanced diet—one that delivers all the necessary daily nutrition needed while providing enough Calories to sustain the energy levels required by travel. Each day you should try to achieve, as best you can, the appropriate amount of carbohydrates, protein, and fat. Better yet, whenever possible, you should try to achieve this balance at each meal. Due to the unpredictability of travel, however, you may have to allow for this balancing to take place over a period of a few days.

You do not need to deprive yourself of any particular food, but you do need to balance out high-Calorie foods taken as part of one meal or snack with low-Calorie foods taken at another time. If you plan to have a rich dessert at dinner, you will have to balance that with an especially low-Calorie food at some other time of the day when you might otherwise have had

THE COMPLETE TRAVEL DIET

a moderate intake of Calories. And try to avoid playing this balancing act in reverse: "I'll spurge now and make up for it tomorrow." That logic is prone to failure because tomorrow never seems to come.

Although it is more important what you eat than when you eat it, if at all possible, try to divide your Calorie consumption into three meals and two to three snacks over the course of each day. Interspersing healthful snacks between meals will keep you satiated and prevent the chance that you will overeat at mealtime. This will provide the best opportunity to consume all the nutrition and Calories you need.

> ### Stress
> Travel today is, if anything, more stressful than in the past. If you allow stress to get the better of you, it can put the double whammy on your plans to lose or maintain your weight while you are traveling.
>
> Stress increases levels of cortisol, which can act to stimulate a craving for carbohydrates often in the form of sweets. What's more, cortisol facilitates the storage of fat on your body. So not only does stress stimulate your appetite, it lures you to high-Calorie foods and then makes it easier for your body to store the excess Calories as fat. Yikes!
>
> Exercise can play a dual role here in helping to burn Calories and at the same time alleviate stress.

Also try to finish your last meal or snack of the day well before bedtime. It's not that your body processes the Calories you consume late at night any differently than it does those during the day. Instead, the problem is that you are more likely to consume foods that are high in fat and Calories (e.g., desserts and alcohol) prior to bedtime.

A special word about breakfast

Your mom was right: Breakfast *is* the most important meal of the day—especially when you are trying to lose weight. Indeed, people who are successful at losing weight share four common behaviors. They eat low-fat, high-carbohydrate diets, they closely monitor their weight, they are physically active, and they eat breakfast.

Without access to your own kitchen while on the road, it can be a challenge to find a café or restaurant serving healthful breakfasts. The "continental breakfast," for instance, has in many cases evolved into little more than a pastry feast. But don't simply skip breakfast thinking that you will consume that many fewer Calories and get a jumpstart on the day's diet. In fact, missing a wholesome breakfast will slow your metabolism as your body tries to conserve energy. This is counter to the result you want if you are trying to lose weight. And when your hunger pangs finally kick in, you may find yourself binging on whatever is available and/or overeating at lunch to try to compensate for the lack of food in your stomach.

Pass up the bacon and eggs and go straight for the whole grain cereals for breakfast. They won't give you the same "taste fix" that the high-fat breakfast foods will, but they will satisfy your hunger and they will "stick to your ribs" so that you won't get hungry again in a few hours.

SIX

Activity
Burning Calories

"Do I really need to exercise when traveling?"

Yes, you do.

"Isn't cutting back on Calories enough?"

No, it isn't

Recall that THE COMPLETE TRAVEL DIET's secret formula includes both eating (less) and moving (more). The simple fact is that if excess Calories aren't burned through physical activity, they will be stored as fat. Regular exercise helps you burn up Calories consumed during the day, as well as extra Calories that have been stored as fat from prior days' excesses that almost always seem to creep into a traveler's eating.

Moreover, exercise can provide a host of health benefits that go well beyond weight loss and maintenance. Regular physical activity can help you prevent disease and improve your overall health. For instance, it may help you to:

- Lower your blood pressure
- Prevent heart disease and stroke
- Avoid back pain
- Prevent osteoporosis
- Prevent or control type 2 diabetes
- Reduce the likelihood of depression
- Improve your ability to manage stress
- Enhance your mood and self-esteem
- Build your strength and tone your muscles

Regular exercise, combined with a healthy diet, is the most efficient and healthful way to control your weight. Did you miss that? Here it is again:

> **Regular exercise, combined with a healthy diet, is the most efficient and healthful way to control your weight!**

If you seek to lose weight while traveling and to keep that weight off after you return from your trip, exercise is as much a contributor to that goal as is modifying your diet.

What's more, if you include regular physical activity in your program to lose weight, you are more likely to keep that weight off when you return home than you would be if you change only your diet while traveling.

An effective diet plan involves more than saying, "No," to large portions and high-Calorie foods. It also includes saying, "Yes," to exercise.

How exercise burns Calories

The physics of Calorie consumption during physical activity are simple. Calories are measures of energy that are expended (i.e., "burned") during work. For the most part, Calories burned are simply a function of your weight and the distance you move.

The basic formula of Calorie consumption is this: Moving 100 pounds a distance equivalent to one mile consumes about 60 Calories.[2] The time it takes to move the 100 pounds that mile plays less of a role. Nevertheless, because it is easier for you, as a traveler, to keep track of time rather than to reckon distances, the table on the next page can give you good approximation of the Calories burned at different "speeds" of movement. It gives some rough estimates of the Calories consumed for activities that are popular with travelers.

So, for instance, if you weigh 180 pounds, you will burn about 108 Calories [60 x 1.8] for each mile that you walk. If you jog or run, you will burn a few extra Calories because more muscle groups are involved in those movements.

---

[2] Walking in-place for the equivalent of one mile—about 2000 steps—consumes the same number of Calories as actually covering a mile although you don't get anywhere.

From this simple equation, you can see that when it comes to the value of exercise in weight loss programs, overweight people have an advantage because they have to do more work to move their bodies the same distance than does a lighter person.

Activity	Calories burned per minute per 100 pounds body weight (approximate)
Slow walking (2 MPH)	2
Golf (No cart)	3.5
Brisk walking (4 MPH)	4
Swimming (Leisurely)	4.5
Jogging (5 MPH)	7
Running (7 MPH)	9.5

Calories burned as a function of weight and time
A more complete list of Calories burned per activity
is available at www.CompleteTravelDiet.com

Keys to being active

As stated in the previous chapter, the keys to a healthy diet are variety, moderation, and balance. The same keys apply to physical activity. If you are active everyday, if you don't overdo it, and if you balance your activity level with your dietary intake, you will succeed at losing weight. The trick is to fit a program of regular physical activity into your travel routine.

Variety

While almost any activity will do, the most easily implemented exercise for travelers is simply walking. Traveling affords lots of opportunities for walking, and unfamiliar scenery wards off the boredom that can come with exercising around the same place day after day. This is where travel provides a real advantage to a dieter.

Besides walking, many hotels have on-site exercise facilities or provide access to nearby health clubs where you can make use of treadmills, stair climbers, stationary bicycles, other aerobic exercise machines, or a swimming pool. Or you may be able to participate in an organized activity of aerobic exercise.

Whatever activity you choose, you should plan to engage in 30 minutes or more of physical activity each day—even on the day's you are in transit. To become more active throughout your travels, take advantage of any chance you get to move around. Look for and welcome all opportunities to add physical activity to your traveling routine.

Moderation

You don't have to run ten miles each day to get the exercise you need. Indeed, the activity you choose does not have to be strenuous to burn off excess Calories. It doesn't even have to come all at the same time. Several short sessions of moderate exercise can be just as effective in burning Calories as one long session.

To be sure, running can provide cardiovascular benefits that walking cannot, and because it uses more muscles groups, running will burn slightly more Calories than walking. But the benefits of simply walking cannot be overlooked. So arrange to

THE COMPLETE TRAVEL DIET

make walking a chief component of your plan to lose weight while on the road.

If you have been sedentary for a while, begin with some easy activities such as walking around the hotel perimeter at a comfortable pace or paddling in the hotel pool. Beginning at a comfortable pace will allow your body to adapt to the increase in your demands of it. Then gradually increase the duration or difficulty of the activity, allowing your body to adapt to each new level. You will find that you will soon able to be more active than you thought possible.

Balance

There are three aspects to the notion of balance in physical activity. First, you must balance the number of Calories you burn while exercising with the number of Calories you consume. If you increase your Calorie consumption, you must increase your physical activity to balance out the weight-gaining effect of your overindulgences.

A second aspect to balance is to weigh the type of activity in which you choose to participate against your current fitness level. Select an activity that isn't too strenuous so that you will be able to participate in it every day, and try to do it every day.

Finally, if you fall just a little short of your activity goal on one day, you *may* be able to balance that out by making up for it on the next day. But don't try to make up for a series of missed activities all at once. The "weekend warrior" approach can set you back rather than catch you up.

SEVEN

Attitude

Developing discipline

THE COMPLETE TRAVEL DIET is not only about how food supplies energy to your body and how your body burns that energy or stores it for future use. It is also about how you think through the decisions you make about what foods to eat and how to use the energy supplied by those foods. You *absolutely* have the ability to succeed in losing weight while traveling and continuing that weight loss after returning home. Whether you *do* succeed, however, depends on the decisions you make, the actions you take, and the attitude you cultivate along the way.

Your formula for reaching your weight loss objectives will be unique and perhaps a little complex. Your current level of fitness, your goals, your eating habits, your travel schedule, and your motivation all come into play. You will have to modify your diet, allocate time to exercise, and monitor your Caloric intake. You may have to change more than a couple of "bad habits" you have picked up while traveling, and you may need to change the whole "style" of your travel. Think of your new dietary plan not as a regime of deprivation but as controlling the fuel for your body. And think of exercise not as tremendous exertion but as simply moving.

THE COMPLETE TRAVEL DIET is about more than just changing your diet and activity levels. It's about changing the way you think about food and exercise. THE COMPLETE TRAVEL DIET is not about "losing 10 pounds by next week." It is about making long-term, permanent, behavioral changes—the kinds of changes that are not easy to make. In fact they are very difficult. But they are not impossible, and if you have the discipline to stick with your plan, you can succeed.

That discipline will be tested along the way—guaranteed. This book can offer you advice and information and maybe set you on your way, but it cannot make the tough choices that you will certainly need to make if you are to be successful. Those have to come from you.

Getting Started

In a way, if you are reading this sentence, you have already started THE COMPLETE TRAVEL DIET. You are at least curious about making changes in your behaviors and routines to help control your weight while traveling. You are starting to frame an attitude that you can travel and control your weight at the same time. You are beginning to believe in the process. And most importantly, you are beginning to believe in yourself.

Now, how do you move from belief to practice? If you wait for the perfect trip to follow THE COMPLETE TRAVEL DIET, you may end up waiting your lifetime because there is no perfect trip. So make your next trip the one where you begin. Here's how.

Do it for yourself

Don't lose weight for anyone other than yourself. Other people may encourage or even intrude upon you to lose weight. A spouse, a friend, an employer, or your physician may wish you to lose weight for reasons of appearance or health. They may even provide incentives to do so. Certainly the encouragement of others is welcome, but the motivation to lose weight must come from within you.

Announce your intentions

Make the commitment. Let everyone know that you intend to maintain your weight or lose weight on your next trip, and that in order to accomplish that goal, you will be making some rather significant changes in the way you travel.

It is especially important to make your intentions clear to any traveling companions, particularly if your behaviors—eating less, moving more—will affect them. For instance, you may choose to begin meetings or tours a little later to allow yourself the time to get a morning walk. Or you may choose to eat dinner at a restaurant serving a healthy selection of foods rather than in your hotel with only a limited menu.

Enlist support

Even if your traveling companions do not share your food selections or your activity routines, their support and encouragement will make it more likely that you will stay on track. Don't count on the support of others, but if it is offered, accept it gratefully.

Overcome roadblocks to starting

There are countless excuses you can find to avoid making changes to your travel habits. Here are just a few.

"I'm too fat."

Nonsense. The fact is that just the opposite is true. The fatter you are, the greater the return you will see from just a few changes in your traveling behavior. Cutting back on Calories and especially just walking 30 minutes a day will have significant impact.

"I might not be able to succeed."

Yep, you might not. Indeed, many people won't. But success and failure are often self-fulfilling predictions. The more you are of the attitude that you will not succeed, the more likely is that outcome. Fortunately, the opposite is true as well. And certainly if you don't try, you are *guaranteed* to fail.

"I don't have time to record the foods I eat."

It's not a matter of time. It's a matter of priority. Many of the same people who claim not to have enough time to keep track of the meals they eat still find the time to keep meticulous records of the frequent flyer points they accumulate.

"Some foods are just too irresistible."

No foods are irresistible. Look around, plenty of people are resisting. It's not the foods that are irresistible; it is your appetite for them.

"I don't have time to exercise when I travel."

Every person who claims not to have time to exercise when traveling doesn't have the same time constraint when it

ATTITUDE

comes to eating. You cannot add hours to the day, but you can prioritize your activities within the time you have.

Remember that exercise does not have to occur in isolation. You can double up with other activities like reviewing a report while using a stationary cycle or listening to a language tape while running on a treadmill.

If you have trouble fitting exercise into your daily routine, get up an hour earlier each day to get in some physical activity before you find yourself locked into doing other things. Another technique is to do more with the time you have. So if you can't walk for 30 minutes, jog for 15. You'll move the same distance and consequently burn the same number of Calories.

"I'm too tired to exercise when I travel"

Exercise increases your blood flow, bringing more oxygen to your muscles and to your brain. Moderate exercise such as a brisk walk can ease the aches you may have from prolonged sitting or confined movement; and instead of tiring you out, it can leave you invigorated. Exercise can also help you get into the rhythm of your destination's time zone and counteract some of the effects of jetlag.

"There's no exercise facility nearby."

No matter where you travel, you can find places to safely walk. Health clubs and gymnasiums are nice hotel bonuses, but they really aren't necessities. If it is equipment that you need, consider packing a jump rope. With a little planning and creativity, you can almost always find a place to exercise—even if it means climbing the stairs in your hotel or walking in place in front of the television set in your hotel room.

THE COMPLETE TRAVEL DIET

"I'm just not motivated."

While incentives can provide necessary rewards along the way, true motivation has to come from within. Your friends and family can offer support, your physician can offer rationale, your scale and mirror can offer you evidence, THE COMPLETE TRAVEL DIET can offer you tips, but only you can supply the motivation.

If you will be exercising by yourself in a secure environment, purchase a wearable radio or CD player to listen to the news or your favorite music while you walk or jog. And if you are looking for some additional motivation, invest in a watch with a stopwatch feature or purchase a pedometer. Keeping track of the duration of your activities or the distances you have covered and setting time and distance goals for the following days will help keep your enthusiasm up.

"Losing weight is incompatible with travel."

Hardly. Weight loss and travel may be a better match than trying to lose weight while operating your normal routine. Being away from home provides an opportunity to try out new low-Calorie foods and to exercise in locations that won't leave you bored.

"Dieting while on vacation is deprivation."

Nothing is prohibited on THE COMPLETE TRAVEL DIET—limited maybe, but not prohibited. Don't focus on the negative, on the foods that are allowed only in small portions. Instead look at all the foods that you can sample. There are many times the numbers of choices of healthy foods as there are unhealthy ones. Focus on what's available and allowable rather than what's prohibited.

ATTITUDE

"I'll start after this trip."

Are you home now? You are? So, have you started your diet?

If you are waiting for the perfect time to begin your diet, you may never start. There will always be another reason (read: excuse) to delay initiating your plan to lose weight. You've probably used one of these excuses yourself:

- *"My next trip is too soon—or too far in the future."*
- *"My next trip is too far away—or too close."*
- *"My next flight is too short—or too long."*
- *...and on and on*

"All these changes seem too weird."

Yes, you may appear a bit eccentric to others—carrying around dried fruit, ordering special restaurant meals, taking walks instead of sitting for a meal. But weigh this against how you will feel when you reach your body weight goal. It will seem that a little eccentricity is a small price to pay.

Continuing

Beginning a diet and exercise program is usually much easier than maintaining it. Your attention is diverted, your motivation wanes, your resolve weakens. How can you persist in working toward the goal you have set?

Set a net daily Calorie goal

Beginning on the first day of your travel, set a net daily Calorie goal for yourself. Then after you have reviewed your log each day, set another goal for the following day. Don't get behind in setting your goal. If you set your goal after you're well into the events of your day, it's likely to be a summary rather than a goal. And don't get ahead of yourself in setting goals for several days in advance, either. Your daily goals should be created in light of your eating and exercise history that is gleaned from the review of your daily logs.

Once you determine what your daily Calorie goal is, record it on your daily Calorie log. (For an example of a daily Calorie log, see page 87.)

Keep daily logs

Every successful diet plan uses some sort of self recording system. Indeed, *one of the most important things you can do to ensure success in reaching your weight loss goal is to keep daily food and activity logs*. This is such an important component to successful weight loss, it bears repeating: ***One of the most important things you can do to ensure success in reaching your weight loss goal is to keep daily food and activity logs***.

Maintaining daily logs of your eating and physical activities requires discipline. You must plot your progress on a nearly hour-by-hour basis. If you are to succeed, the completion of your logs on a timely basis is essential.

The logs you use do not have to be elaborate, but they do have to allow for an accurate accounting of the Calories you take in and the Calories you burn off each day. Make sure it is easy to enter information into your daily logs and that they are readily accessible.

Sample daily food and activity logs are provided in this chapter. The logs are also available for download from THE COMPLETE TRAVEL DIET Web site at www.CompleteTravelDiet.com. You can make copies of these pages and use them as is, or you can make up your own logs. No matter how you decide to put together your food and activity logs, they should be portable,

ATTITUDE

and whenever possible, you should keep them with you from the time you rise in the morning until you retire for the evening.

Daily food log

The daily food log on page 84 shows several columns. The first column is to record each food item consumed. The next columns are arranged from left-to-right in relationship, more or less, with the Food Guide Pyramid's layout from bottom-to-top. Notice that more than one column is available for recording servings from the dairy and protein food groups. That's because "whole fat" dairy foods have about twice the Calorie content as "fat-free" dairy foods, and because "fatty" protein food items have about three times as many Calories as "lean" protein foods.

At the bottom of the food group columns are the approximate Calorie counts for one serving from that food group. As you go about your travels, record each food item you eat and the number of servings eaten in the appropriate columns. (Examples of daily food logs, completed on a per-meal basis are given on pages 100 – 111 and 118 – 129 in the next chapter.)

At the conclusion of each meal, or at the end of each day, total the number of servings from each column and multiply that total by the appropriate food group Calorie count. Then add all the Calories together to arrive at the approximate total number Calories you consumed in that meal or in that day.

As a quick determinant of the balance in your diet, look at the distribution of servings across the columns. At the end of each day you should see more marks in the three leftmost columns with fewer marks as you scan to the right, and with (ideally) no marks in the farthest rightmost column.

THE COMPLETE TRAVEL DIET

Daily food log for _____

Food	Starch	Vegetable	Fruit	Dairy (whole)	Dairy (non)	Protein (fatty)	Protein (med)	Protein (lean)	Junk
Servings									
Calorie multipliers	80	25	60	150	80	225	165	75	50
Food group Calories									
Total Calories consumed									

ATTITUDE

Daily activity log for _____

Activity	Minutes	Multi-plier	Calories
Activity Calories (Sum Calories column)			
Weight factor (Your weight X .01)			
Total Calories burned (Activity Calories X Weight factor)			

The Complete Travel Diet

Daily activity log

To determine whether your body is adding or losing fat, you must record not only the Calories you consume in a day but also the Calories you expend. To do that, use a daily activity log like the one on the previous page. In it, list each significant physical activity in which you participate in the course of a day. Next to that, write down the duration of each of those activities. In the "Multiplier" column use a value selected from the table on page 72. In the last column, put the result of the "Minutes" column multiplied by the "Multiplier" column. Then total the "Calories" column, multiply that value by your weight, then by .01, and record that value as "Total Calories burned." (Examples of these are shown on pages 112 – 113 and 130 – 131.)

Daily Calorie log

To find out your net daily Calorie consumption, reconcile the Calories you put into your body with the Calories you burned off through exercise. Completing a daily Calorie log like the one on page 87 is a way to help you do just that. Subtracting the Calories you burned off through exercise from the Calories you took in through eating, then comparing the result with your net daily Calorie goal, you will have a clear and incontrovertible picture of whether or not you are on the path to reaching your ultimate body weight goal.

Expect that your net daily Calorie consumption will rarely hit your daily Calorie goal exactly. After all, traveling is unpredictable and it is only natural that you will overdo it in some areas and underdo it in others. Even if they do match exactly, both values are inexact approximations that should be used only to reveal relative progress and trends.

ATTITUDE

Daily Calorie log for _____

Summary	Calories
Calories consumed	
Breakfast	
Mid-morning snack	
Lunch	
Mid-afternoon snack	
Dinner	
Evening snack	
Other	
Total Calories consumed	
Calories spent [from activity log]	( )
Net daily Calories	
Net Calorie goal >>>>>>>>>>>>>>>>	
Progress?	

Review your logs

Your daily logs are more than records of Calories consumed and burned. As chronicles of your behavior, they are valuable tools to help you learn more about the food choices you make and the exercising routines you follow. A review of your eating habits and physical activities can point to areas where you may be able to improve your food selections or exercise options.

Look to your logs for clues to the circumstances that lead you to imprudent food selections or to not enough time spent in physical activities. If you discover such patterns, work to dissociate those activities from your eating or exercise patterns. For instance, you may discover that you often eat too much junk food while waiting to connect between airplane flights. In this case you could pack some meal replacement bars to eat between flights in the future. Likewise, if you notice that you are more faithful to an exercise routine that is completed in the morning, avoid trying to fit in your exercises in the afternoon or evening.

You should use the review of each day's logs as information to help you modify your behavior to reach your ultimate goal, not change your goal to match your behavior. Your current daily net Calorie goal should be based on, but independent of your behavior that is represented in the results of previous days' logs. If, for instance, you carry over a missed goal from a previous day, you will be brought down by the "failure" of yesterday, and you will be tempted to adjust your current daily net Calorie goal to "make up for yesterday." Don't. Stick with your plan and see it through.

Most importantly, carry your logs with you on your trip and record *everything*—everything you eat, everything you

ATTITUDE

drink, and every minute you exercise. Don't cheat when recording in your log.

Slips and stumbles

If you slip—and you will, especially with the unpredictabilities of travel—the time to test your resolve will have arrived. This is a critical time in determining the success you will have in reaching your goals. No other time tests your will and motivation than does a setback in your progress in reaching your goal. This is also the point where most people quit.

But a slip is just that: A temporary setback from which you not only can recover but can learn. Instead of feeling bad about the setback or worse, abandoning your plan, use the experience to better deal with similar situations in which you may find yourself in the future.

Acknowledge it

Don't pretend that the slip didn't happen. It did, and you did it. You ate too much of the wrong food. You took a taxi when you could have walked instead. Denial will only allow you to repeat the mistake.

Accept responsibility

Unless you were kidnapped, forced to eat something you had not intended, and locked in a room, you can blame no one but yourself for your stumble. You are responsible for your health and fitness—nobody else.

Don't beat yourself up

You will have a setback or two. Everyone will. The only thing that you are guilty of is being human, so don't wrap yourself in blame. Your energy will be better spent looking rationally at what happened to make you stumble and fixing your plan to prevent it from happening again. Use the incident as a

THE COMPLETE TRAVEL DIET

learning experience. If you can recover quickly, without beating yourself up for your lapse, you will become more determined and more likely to succeed.

Don't ignore your behavior

There is a chance here to learn from your mistake. What caused the slip? Did you delay a meal too long? Did you choose to sleep-in instead of arising for an early morning jog? Did you go along with the crowd so as to not feel out of place?

Forget about the effect of your overindulgence or your missed activity and focus on the cause of it.

Focus on preceding events

If you concentrate on your (failed) behavior, you are more likely to give up. However if you concentrate on what the events were that lead up to that behavior, this becomes a learning experience, and you can use it to make changes to your plan. Then the next time you see these events looming, you will be able to make more sensible choices.

Avoid the scene of the crime

Don't return to the same restaurant or even order the same meal to prove that you can correct the error of your ways. Reconstructing the scene where you had a setback may encourage you to eat less than you should, or its association with your setback will at least make the eating experience less pleasant.

Curiously, for some people the opposite approach can sometimes be an effective technique too. That is, return to face your dietary nemesis head on. For instance, if you find that you can't seem to pass up an ice cream shop in an airport or the free continental breakfast at your hotel, make it a point to find your way to an airport ice cream shop or the hotel breakfast bar for a good look. Then turn away for a healthier choice.

But be careful of this tactic. If you plan to use it, you had better have a healthier alternative already identified and be able to move to it straight away.

Update your plan

You must revise your eating/exercise plan to account for the mistake you made. Perhaps select different restaurants. Perhaps exercise an extra 20 minutes. Use your analysis of the causes to re-jiggle your plan to eliminate the events or surrounding circumstances that were responsible for your setback.

Get back to your plan

Sure you want to balance the Calories you consume and the Calories you burn over a period of days, but don't try to make up for a major overindulgence by starving yourself for the next day or two, and don't attempt to double or triple your level of activity if you missed a couple of days. You will hate the punishment and only interfere with your ability to get back to your plan. If that plan is a sound one, it will see you through.

Getting unstuck

You can follow all the advice of THE COMPLETE TRAVEL DIET and still not lose an ounce on your next trip. In fact, you could even gain weight—especially if you have increased the physical activity component of your regimen wherein you are replacing stored fat with denser muscle fiber. In that case, you are not stuck at all.

Likewise, if you are conscientiously cutting back on your Calories and expending more energy through exercise and still seem to be stuck on a plateau, it is probably just that: A plateau. Even if you are consistent in your eating habits and physical activity, your weight will naturally vary from day to day and week to week. Weight loss (or for that matter, weight gain)

THE COMPLETE TRAVEL DIET

does not follow a straight line down (or up). From time-to-time that line will flatten out.

Stick with your plan. Don't cut back on Calories. You can't break through a weight loss plateau by reducing your Calorie consumption even more. In fact, if you put your body in starvation mode, it will adjust to conserve every Calorie it gets. If you want to make an adjustment to your plan, step up your physical activity a little. Walk a little longer or more frequently, for instance. This will keep your body's metabolic rate up.

Keep true to your plan. You have more discipline than you think. It's interesting to observe how much discipline overweight people seem to muster following their release from a hospital after suffering a heart attack or other serious weight-related illness. They muster the discipline and so can you. The challenge is to maintain it. If you do, it will pay off.

How to say "No"

It can be difficult, particularly in a business situation, to say "no" when offered the wrong kinds of food or too much of it. You don't want to insult the offerer or give the impression that the food you are offered—particularly in a different culture—is offensive to you. So what do you do? Having a repertoire of responses in place ahead of time can take the pressure off. Here are some ways to refuse without insult.

- *"My stomach is a bit sensitive. I may have picked up a little bug on this trip."*
- *"I'm feeling a little under the weather."*
- *"Sorry, I can't. Doctor's orders"*

Announcing, "I'm on a diet," although truthful, may not be the best approach. Others at the table, perhaps feeling a little guilty about their own eating and exercise habits, may try to dissuade you from sticking to your plan, or make light of your endeavor. In any event the conversation is likely to turn to diet, food, eating, and the like. Just the kind of conversation you could do better avoiding.

Food cravings

What triggers a craving is not entirely clear. Cravings may have a physiological basis—for instance sweets may alter your mood by causing the release of serotonin or endorphins. Or they may be learned—you have found that eating certain foods has "made you feel better."

A mid-afternoon craving for a candy bar or a bag of chips may be your body's signal that it has been too long since you last ate, or it may be that you have developed a habit of seeking out a snack in the afternoon, or both. (It's often hard to tell which is which.) Regardless of the causes, cravings can make dieting difficult, especially when a traveler can find food on almost every corner.

If it were a perfect system, you would crave foods that contained nutrients that your body needed. But when was the last time you craved spinach or Brussels sprouts? Instead, through the years, poor eating habits and social conditioning have conspired with your physiology so that you are more likely to crave high-Calorie or high-fat foods that have little nutritional value.

What you can do

First recognize that this is likely a craving—a circumstance that is not the same as hunger. If you are hungry, you seek Calories. If instead you are seeking a particular food (e.g., potato chips) or food type (e.g., sweets), you are most likely "craving."

A craving could also be a need to satisfy the activity of eating. In such a case, it could be that you are bored, or it might

THE COMPLETE TRAVEL DIET

be that you are angry, upset, or in another heightened state of emotion.

Try to determine the source of the craving. Do you get the same cravings at a particular time of day (e.g., afternoon), after a particular activity (e.g., an airplane ride), in a particular location (e.g., an airport), after experiencing a particular emotion (e.g., anxiety, frustration, loneliness—all of which can be experienced when traveling), or when encountering a particular odor (e.g., bakery)? If you can determine what triggers your cravings you may be able to modify your travel plans to avoid those circumstances.

Once you have identified your desire for food as a craving, delay gratifying it. (You are not denying; you are delaying.) First delay it by just a few minutes, working up to several minutes. By the time you are able to delay satisfying a craving by an hour, you will probably no longer have it.

Here are some other techniques.

- Exercise – This hits cravings with a double whammy. First, it can redirect your mind away from food. (People who exercise sometimes think about eating while they are involved in their physical activity, but that subject does not typically pervade their thinking.) Secondly, when you substitute exercise for succumbing to your craving, you will be burning rather than storing Calories.

- Substitute a food item – Instead of potato chips, try baked tortilla chips. Instead of ice cream, choose fat-free, sugar-free ice cream or frozen yogurt.

- Substitute an activity – Shop, take in a movie, take a tour. Travel often provides many opportunities to do something else.

ATTITUDE

- **Substitute food types** – If you crave sugar, for instance, take the sugar in a healthful food such as fruit rather than packaged snacks. At least you will be getting other nutrients and some fiber.

- **Drink water** – This will put something in your stomach for a time, thus removing one of the signals you may be receiving that contributes to your craving.

- **Give in** – It is not the end of the world, and sometimes it just feels awfully darn good. But exercise moderation. Make the portion half as large as you normally would. Then get on with your itinerary.

- **Create a distraction** – When a craving hits, by definition it preoccupies your mind. The good news is that it is a transient experience. If you can distract yourself for a few minutes, the craving will pass. So instead of giving in, redirect your attention by reviewing your itinerary or by preparing for a business meeting or by taking a walk around the block. (Try to avoid passing too many restaurants.) You'll feel that you accomplished something and may even get in some exercise. Most importantly, you will have allowed time for the craving to pass.

- **Develop a "tart tooth"** – If you have a "sweet tooth" or crave sweets, switch from foods containing refined sugars to foods containing fructose (i.e., fruit) sugars. After a few months of less processed sugar in your diet, your intestines, your body, and your mood get used to the more comfortable after-meal feeling of complex carbohydrates. Eventually, you will shun candy bars and sugar-sweetened foods and will be put-off by how you feel if you eat a packaged sweet treat, especially one that is squarely in the junk food category.

Once your tongue gets used to a tarter taste, you're well on your way to enjoying a healthier relationship with the sugars in your life. Eventually, as your body becomes wiser, you will crave what's good for you.

- Finally—you'll see why I kept this suggestion for last—gargle with an antiseptic mouthwash. That will sidetrack your taste buds for sure.

Give yourself time to adjust. Like other habits, food cravings take time to develop and, likewise, time to fade away.

EIGHT

Model plans

Sample regimens

The considerable diversity among people combined with the extensive variabilities of travel makes it impossible to prescribe a diet and exercise plan that applies universally. Instead, included in this chapter are two case studies.

The first case compares the daily Calorie logs of two traveling businesswomen, who are matched in height, weight, and age, but who differ in eating and exercise patterns. The second case study similarly compares the daily Calorie logs of two men traveling on vacation who are likewise matched in height, weight, and age and also differ in eating and exercise practices.

THE COMPLETE TRAVEL DIET

Case one: Traveling businesswomen

Two women of equal age and stature are traveling on one-week business trips. Each is 34 years old, 5 feet 4 inches tall, and weighs 155 pounds, which results in a BMR[3] of 1460 Calories for each woman.

The first of this pair—we'll call her *Jane*—has no weight loss plans while traveling. She will follow the dietary and exercise routine she normally follows while traveling, which is "lightly active."

The other woman, *Mary*, has decided that she needs to shed a few pounds. She has a body weight goal of 135 pounds, which she expects to achieve over the next few months. This will bring her BMI well within the "normal" weight status range. Mary has decided to follow THE COMPLETE TRAVEL DIET during her trip as a way to begin to change her eating habits and exercise routine.

Mary's goal

The first thing Mary has to do is determine how much weight she wants to lose per week toward her ultimate body weight goal of 135 pounds.

As discussed in Chapter Three, her goal should be to lose between ½ to 2 pounds per week, but no more than 1% of her current weight. Mary decides to shoot for the maximum recommended—in her case, about 1½ pounds.

---

[3] BMR = 655 + (4.3 × BODY WEIGHT IN POUNDS) + (4.7 × HEIGHT IN INCHES) - (4.7 × AGE IN YEARS).

Mary's plan

Mary's plan to reach her goal will be based on two factors: Her activity adjusted BMR (see pages 16 and 17), and the one pound rule (page 39).

Both women's BMR is 1460 Calories—the minimum number of Calories they should consume daily. Mary generally keeps "moderately active" while traveling so her activity adjusted BMR is 2190 Calories [1.5 x 1460], the daily Calories needed to maintain her weight for her height, age, and activity level.

Serving estimates

Calories derived from the USDA's National Nutrient Database are shown in brackets [ ] on each case study's food and activity logs so that you can compare the actual to the estimated Calories of each food item.

You are not expected to provide actual Calorie data in your logs. Indeed, that's the point of using serving estimates.

But Mary wants to lose 1½ pounds by the time she returns from her week-long trip. That 1½ pounds works out to be a net loss of 5250 Calories [1½ x 3500] over the course of the week—about 750 Calories per day. That would reduce her daily net Calorie consumption to 1440 [2190 – 750]. But Mary must eat at least 1460 Calories per day to fulfill her BMR requirement. Consequently, she will have to increase her exercise regimen along with watching her Calorie intake.

Daily Calorie logs

Daily food and activity logs for Jane and Mary are shown side-by-side on the following pages. The logs are the same daily food and activity logs provided for you on pages 84 and 85.

THE COMPLETE TRAVEL DIET

Jane's breakfast

Food	Starch	Vegetable	Fruit	Dairy (whole)	Dairy (non)	Protein (fatty)	Protein (med)	Protein (lean)	Junk
Orange juice (1 cup) [110]			//						
Almond Danish pastry [280]	/								/
Butter [72]				/					
Coffee [5]									
Sugar (1 tsp) [16]									/
Creamer (1 tsp) [15]									/
Servings	*1*		*2*	*1*					*3*
Calorie multipliers	80	25	60	150	80	225	165	75	50
Food group Calories	*80*		*120*	*150*					*150*
Total Calories consumed					*500*				

MODEL PLANS

Mary's breakfast

Food	Starch	Vegetable	Fruit	Dairy (whole)	Dairy (non)	Protein (fatty)	Protein (med)	Protein (lean)	Junk
Water (1 cup)									
Orange juice (1 cup) [110]			//						
Oatmeal (1 cup) [109]	//								
Skim milk ($\frac{1}{2}$ cup) [43]					/				
Coffee [5]									
Servings	2		2		1				
Calorie multipliers	80	25	60	150	80	225	165	75	50
Food group Calories	160		120		80				
Total Calories consumed	360								

THE COMPLETE TRAVEL DIET

Jane's mid-morning snack

Food	Starch	Vegetable	Fruit	Dairy (whole)	Dairy (non)	Protein (fatty)	Protein (med)	Protein (lean)	Junk
Fruit and cereal bar (2) [220]	//								/
Coffee [5]									
Sugar (1 tsp) [16]									/
Creamer (1 tsp) [15]									/
Servings	2								3
Calorie multipliers	80	25	60	150	80	225	165	75	50
Food group Calories	160								150
Total Calories consumed	\multicolumn{9}{c}{310}

MODEL PLANS

Mary's mid-morning snack

Food	Starch	Vegetable	Fruit	Dairy (whole)	Dairy (non)	Protein (fatty)	Protein (med)	Protein (lean)	Junk
Water (1 cup)									
Banana [138]			//						
Coffee [5]									
Servings			2						
Calorie multipliers	80	25	60	150	80	225	165	75	50
Food group Calories			120						
Total Calories consumed					120				

THE COMPLETE TRAVEL DIET

Jane's fast-food lunch

Food	Starch	Vegetable	Fruit	Dairy (whole)	Dairy (non)	Protein (fatty)	Protein (med)	Protein (lean)	Junk
Cheeseburger (single) [359]	//	/		/			/		
French fries (small) [291]	/								//
Ketchup [20]									/
Cola (medium) [152]									//
Servings	3	1		1			1		5
Calorie multipliers	80	25	60	150	80	225	165	75	50
Food group Calories	240	25		150			165		250
Total Calories consumed					830				

MODEL PLANS

Mary's fast-food lunch

Food	Starch	Vegetable	Fruit	Dairy (whole)	Dairy (non)	Protein (fatty)	Protein (med)	Protein (lean)	Junk
Water (1 cup)									
½ Tuna sub on wheat [292]	//							/	/
Potato salad (½ cup) [163]	/								/
Choc ice cream (½ cup) [143]				/					
Servings	3			1				1	2
Calorie multipliers	80	25	60	150	80	225	165	75	50
Food group Calories	240			150				75	100
Total Calories consumed	\multicolumn{9}{c}{565}

105

THE COMPLETE TRAVEL DIET

Jane's afternoon snack

Food	Starch	Vegetable	Fruit	Dairy (whole)	Dairy (non)	Protein (fatty)	Protein (med)	Protein (lean)	Junk
Chocolate bar [198]									////
Cola (medium) [152]									//
Servings									6
Calorie multipliers	80	25	60	150	80	225	165	75	50
Food group Calories									300
Total Calories consumed	300								

Mary's afternoon snack

Food	Starch	Vegetable	Fruit	Dairy (whole)	Dairy (non)	Protein (fatty)	Protein (med)	Protein (lean)	Junk
Water (1 cup)									
Roasted pistachios (2 oz) [322]						1			
Diet cola (medium) [4]									
Servings						*1*			
Calorie multipliers	80	25	60	150	80	225	165	75	50
Food group Calories						*225*			
Total Calories consumed	*225*								

Jane's dinner

Food	Starch	Vegetable	Fruit	Dairy (whole)	Dairy (non)	Protein (fatty)	Protein (med)	Protein (lean)	Junk
Wine (1 glass, Burgundy) [72]									/
Salad (¾ cup) [17]		/							
Roquefort dressing [152]				/					
Prime rib [570]						//			
Mushrooms [21]		/							
Asparagus [70]		/							
Hollandaise sauce [188]				/					/
Vanilla ice cream (½ cup) [145]				/					
Coffee (1 cup) [5]									
Sugar (1 tsp) [16]									/
Creamer (1 tsp) [15]									/
Servings		3		3		2			4
Calorie multipliers	80	25	60	150	80	225	165	75	50
Food group Calories		75		450		450			200
Total Calories consumed					1175				

MODEL PLANS

Mary's dinner

Food	Starch	Vegetable	Fruit	Dairy (whole)	Dairy (non)	Protein (fatty)	Protein (med)	Protein (lean)	Junk
Water (1 cup)									
Wine (1 glass, Chardonnay) [68]									/
Salad ($\frac{3}{4}$ cup) [17]		/							
Low-Cal Italian dressing [16]									/
Pasta [148]	//								
Marinara sauce [71]		/							/
Cantaloupe ($\frac{1}{2}$ cup) [28]			/						
Coffee (1 cup) [5]									
Servings	2	2	1						3
Calorie multipliers	80	25	60	150	80	225	165	75	50
Food group Calories	160	50	60						150
Total Calories consumed	\multicolumn{9}{c}{420}

THE COMPLETE TRAVEL DIET

Jane's evening snack

Food	Starch	Vegetable	Fruit	Dairy (whole)	Dairy (non)	Protein (fatty)	Protein (med)	Protein (lean)	Junk
Sherry (4 oz) [180]									//
Servings									2
Calorie multipliers	80	25	60	150	80	225	165	75	50
Food group Calories									100
Total Calories consumed	100

Mary's evening snack

Food	Starch	Vegetable	Fruit	Dairy (whole)	Dairy (non)	Protein (fatty)	Protein (med)	Protein (lean)	Junk
Water (1 cup)									
Apple (medium) [62]			1						
Servings			1						
Calorie multipliers	80	25	60	150	80	225	165	75	50
Food group Calories			60						
Total Calories consumed	\multicolumn{9}{c}{60}

THE COMPLETE TRAVEL DIET

Jane's daily activity log

Activity	Minutes	Multi-plier	Calories
Slow walk with clients during meeting break	15	2	30
Slow walk back to hotel from client meeting	20	2	40
After dinner walk to local mall	50	*	
*Jane should record all her activities. However those that are part of her normal routine (i.e., those activities that make her a "lightly active" person) cannot be counted as <u>additional</u> Calorie-burning activities in her log.			
Activity Calories (Sum Calories column)			70
Weight factor (Your weight X .01)			1.5
Total Calories burned (Activity Calories X Weight factor)			105

112

MODEL PLANS

Mary's daily activity log

Activity	Minutes	Multi-plier	Calories
Jog on hotel treadmill	30	7	210
Brisk walk to/from client meeting	15	*	
Slow walk during meeting break	10	*	
Slow walk during lunch break	20	*	
Brisk walk to/from restaurant	15	4	60
Swim in hotel pool	15	*	
*Mary should record all her activities. However those that are part of her normal routine (i.e., those activities that make her a "moderately active" person) cannot be counted as <u>additional</u> Calorie-burning activities in her log.			
Activity Calories (Sum Calories column)			270
Weight factor (Your weight X .01)			1.5
Total Calories burned (Activity Calories X Weight factor)			405

Jane's daily Calorie log

Summary	Calories
Calories consumed	
Breakfast	500
Mid-morning snack	310
Lunch	830
Mid-afternoon snack	300
Dinner	1175
Evening snack	100
Other	
Total Calories consumed	3215
Calories spent [from activity log]	(105)
Net daily Calories	3110
Net Calorie goal >>>>>>>>>>>>>>>>	---
Progress?	

Mary's daily Calorie log

Summary	Calories
Calories consumed	
Breakfast	360
Mid-morning snack	120
Lunch	565
Mid-afternoon snack	225
Dinner	420
Evening snack	60
Other	
Total Calories consumed	1750
Calories spent [from activity log]	(405)
Net daily Calories	1345
Net Calorie goal >>>>>>>>>>>>>>>	1440
Progress?	Yeah!

THE COMPLETE TRAVEL DIET

Case two: Vacationing men

Similar to the first case study of Jane and Mary, this case tracks the diet and exercise schedules for two men traveling on vacation. Each man is 45 years-old, 5 feet 11 inches tall, and weighs 205 pounds. Their BMRs[4] are 1970 Calories.

Like Jane, the first man has no plans to control his Caloric intake or to partake of much exercise at all during his two-week vacation. We'll call him *Joe*.

Max, the other man in this case study, is also vacationing for two weeks. Unlike Joe, however, Max has decided to use his vacation to improve his health. He has a BMI that puts him in the "overweight" category… and he feels it. So Max has set for himself a body weight goal of 175 pounds. This will bring Max's BMI into the "normal" range.

Like Mary, in the first case study, Max intends to reach his weight goal over the next few months but will begin to change his eating habits and exercise routine while on vacation by following THE COMPLETE TRAVEL DIET.

Max's goal

To reach his ultimate goal of losing 30 pounds, Max has to decide how much weight he wants to lose per week but should aim for between a ½ to 2 pound weight loss for each of the two weeks he will be on vacation—as well as for the remaining weeks he works toward that goal.

---

[4] BMR = 66 + (6.3 X BODY WEIGHT IN POUNDS) + (12.9 X HEIGHT IN INCHES) - (6.8 X AGE IN YEARS).

MODEL PLANS

Max knows himself and knows that trying to lose 4 pounds by the time he returns may be too ambitious. So he decides to make his weekly weight loss goal an easily attainable 1 pound.

Max's plan

Max's plan to reach his goal of shedding 2 pounds by the time he returns from his vacation is pinned on the same two factors as is Mary's plan—and as your plan will be too: His activity adjusted BMR and the one pound rule.

As noted, Max's BMR is 1970 Calories—the minimum number of Calories he should consume daily. Max doesn't exercise regularly while traveling. In fact he doesn't exercise regularly at all. So Max's activity adjusted BMR is 2360 Calories—the daily Calories needed to sustain his weight for his height, age, and "sedentary" activity level (see page 17).

For Max to lose 2 pounds by the time he returns from his two-week vacation, he will have to incur a net loss of 7000 Calories [2 x 3500] or an average of 500 Calories per day. That means that Max will have to reduce his daily net Calorie consumption to 1860 [2360 - 500]. Because Max should not cut his Caloric intake below his BMR of 1970, he will have to begin a program of regular exercise to burn off *at least* 100 extra Calories per day.

Daily Calorie logs

Daily food and exercise logs for Joe and Max are shown side-by-side on the following pages.

THE COMPLETE TRAVEL DIET

Joe's breakfast

Food	Starch	Vegetable	Fruit	Dairy (whole)	Dairy (non)	Protein (fatty)	Protein (med)	Protein (lean)	Junk
Orange juice (1 cup) [110]			//						
Omelet (3 eggs) [279]								///	
Onion [10]		/							
Bacon [73]						/			
Cheese [246]				//					
Wheat toast (2 slices) [138]	//								
Butter [72]				/					
Jam [78]									/
Coffee [5]									
Sugar (1 tsp) [16]									/
Creamer (1 tsp) [15]									/
Servings	2	1	2	3		1		3	3
Calorie multipliers	80	25	60	150	80	225	165	75	50
Food group Calories	160	25	120	450		225		225	150
Total Calories consumed	\multicolumn{9}{c}{1355}

118

MODEL PLANS

Max's breakfast

Food	Starch	Vegetable	Fruit	Dairy (whole)	Dairy (non)	Protein (fatty)	Protein (med)	Protein (lean)	Junk
Water (1 cup)									
Orange juice (1 cup) [110]			//						
Oatmeal (1 cup) [109]	//								
Skim milk ($\frac{1}{2}$ cup) [43]					/				
Wheat toast (2 slices) [138]	//								
Coffee [5]									
Servings	4		2		1				
Calorie multipliers	80	25	60	150	80	225	165	75	50
Food group Calories	320		120		80				
Total Calories consumed	\multicolumn{9}{c}{520}

THE COMPLETE TRAVEL DIET

Joe's mid-morning snack

Food	Starch	Vegetable	Fruit	Dairy (whole)	Dairy (non)	Protein (fatty)	Protein (med)	Protein (lean)	Junk
Chocolate chip cookies (2) [260]									////
Coffee [5]									
Sugar (1 tsp) [16]									/
Creamer (1 tsp) [15]									/
Servings									6
Calorie multipliers	80	25	60	150	80	225	165	75	50
Food group Calories									300
Total Calories consumed	300									

MODEL PLANS

Max's mid-morning snack

Food	Starch	Vegetable	Fruit	Dairy (whole)	Dairy (non)	Protein (fatty)	Protein (med)	Protein (lean)	Junk
Water (1 cup)									
Banana [138]			//						
Coffee [5]									
Servings			2						
Calorie multipliers	80	25	60	150	80	225	165	75	50
Food group Calories			120						
Total Calories consumed					120				

THE COMPLETE TRAVEL DIET

Joe's fast-food lunch

Food	Starch	Vegetable	Fruit	Dairy (whole)	Dairy (non)	Protein (fatty)	Protein (med)	Protein (lean)	Junk
Cheeseburger (single) [359]	//	/		/			/		
Onion rings (medium) [244]		/							//
Ketchup [20]									/
Cola (medium) [152]									//
Servings	2	2		1			1		5
Calorie multipliers	80	25	60	150	80	225	165	75	50
Food group Calories	160	50		150			165		250
Total Calories consumed	\multicolumn{9}{c}{775}

MODEL PLANS

Max's fast-food lunch

Food	Starch	Vegetable	Fruit	Dairy (whole)	Dairy (non)	Protein (fatty)	Protein (med)	Protein (lean)	Junk
Water (1 cup)									
Turkey sandwich on wheat [277]	//							/	
Mustard [3]									
Low-fat cheese [98]					/				
Potato salad (½ cup) [163]	/							/	
Skim milk (1 cup) [86]					//				
Orange [64]			/						
Servings	3		1		3			2	
Calorie multipliers	80	25	60	150	80	225	165	75	50
Food group Calories	240		60		240			150	
Total Calories consumed	\multicolumn{9}{c}{690}

Total Calories consumed: 690

THE COMPLETE TRAVEL DIET

Joe's afternoon snack

Food	Starch	Vegetable	Fruit	Dairy (whole)	Dairy (non)	Protein (fatty)	Protein (med)	Protein (lean)	Junk
Potato chips (2 oz. bag) [304]	/								////
Cola (medium) [152]									//
Servings	1								6
Calorie multipliers	80	25	60	150	80	225	165	75	50
Food group Calories	80								300
Total Calories consumed					380				

MODEL PLANS

Max's afternoon snack

Food	Starch	Vegetable	Fruit	Dairy (whole)	Dairy (non)	Protein (fatty)	Protein (med)	Protein (lean)	Junk
Water (1 cup)									
Air-popped popcorn (1 cup) [31]		1							
Diet cola (medium) [4]									
Peach (medium) [42]			1						
Servings		1	1						
Calorie multipliers	80	25	60	150	80	225	165	75	50
Food group Calories		25	60						
Total Calories consumed					85				

THE COMPLETE TRAVEL DIET

Joe's dinner

Food	Starch	Vegetable	Fruit	Dairy (whole)	Dairy (non)	Protein (fatty)	Protein (med)	Protein (lean)	Junk
Wine (1 glass, Burgundy) [72]									/
Salad (1½ cups) [35]		//							
Roquefort dressing [152]				/					
Prime rib [570]						//			
Mushrooms [21]		/							
Asparagus [70]		/							
Hollandaise sauce [188]				/					/
Baked potato (medium) [93]	/								
Sour cream [52]				/					
Butter [102]				/					
Cheesecake [257]									//
Coffee (1 cup) [5]									
Sugar (1 tsp) [16]									/
Creamer (1 tsp) [15]									/
Servings	1	4		4		2			6
Calorie multipliers	80	25	60	150	80	225	165	75	50
Food group Calories	80	100		600		450			300
Total Calories consumed	\multicolumn{9}{c	}{1530}

126

Model plans

Max's dinner

Food	Starch	Vegetable	Fruit	Dairy (whole)	Dairy (non)	Protein (fatty)	Protein (med)	Protein (lean)	Junk
Water (1 cup)									
Wine (1 glass, Chardonnay) [68]									/
Salad (1½ cups) [35]		//							
Low-Cal Italian dressing [16]									/
Pasta [148]	//								
Marinara sauce [71]		/							/
Sourdough bread (1 slice) [129]	/								
Fresh strawberries (½ cup) [84]			/						
Coffee (1 cup) [5]									
Servings	3	3	1						3
Calorie multipliers	80	25	60	150	80	225	165	75	50
Food group Calories	240	75	60						150
Total Calories consumed	\multicolumn{9}{c}{525}

THE COMPLETE TRAVEL DIET

Joe's evening snack

Food	Starch	Vegetable	Fruit	Dairy (whole)	Dairy (non)	Protein (fatty)	Protein (med)	Protein (lean)	Junk
Sherry (4 oz) [180]									//
Servings									2
Calorie multipliers	80	25	60	150	80	225	165	75	50
Food group Calories									100
Total Calories consumed	100

MODEL PLANS

Max's evening snack

Food	Starch	Vegetable	Fruit	Dairy (whole)	Dairy (non)	Protein (fatty)	Protein (med)	Protein (lean)	Junk
Water (1 cup)									
Apple (medium) [62]			1						
Servings			1						
Calorie multipliers	80	25	60	150	80	225	165	75	50
Food group Calories			60						
Total Calories consumed	60								

THE COMPLETE TRAVEL DIET

Joe's daily activity log

Activity	Minutes	Multi-plier	Calories
Slow walk between gates in airport	10	2	20
Slow walk from train station to hotel	5	2	10
Activity Calories (Sum Calories column)			30
Weight factor (Your weight X .01)			2
Total Calories burned (Activity Calories X Weight factor)			60

Max's daily activity log

Activity	Minutes	Multi-plier	Calories
Slow walk to/from coffee shop for breakfast	15	2	30
Slow walking tour of village	40	2	80
Brisk walk after dinner	20	4	80
Activity Calories (Sum Calories column)			190
Weight factor (Your weight X .01)			2
Total Calories burned (Activity Calories X Weight factor)			380

Joe's daily Calorie log

Summary	Calories
Calories consumed	
Breakfast	1355
Mid-morning snack	300
Lunch	775
Mid-afternoon snack	380
Dinner	1530
Evening snack	100
Other	
Total Calories consumed	4440
Calories spent [from activity log]	(60)
Net daily Calories	4380
Net Calorie goal >>>>>>>>>>>>>>>>	---
Progress?	---

Max's daily Calorie log

Summary	Calories
Calories consumed	
Breakfast	520
Mid-morning snack	120
Lunch	690
Mid-afternoon snack	85
Dinner	525
Evening snack	60
Other	
Total Calories consumed	2000
Calories spent [from activity log]	(380)
Net daily Calories	1620
Net Calorie goal >>>>>>>>>>>>>>>	1860
Progress?	Great!

THE COMPLETE TRAVEL DIET

Case study synopses

After one day, here is how the Calories added up for our four travelers. (For Jane and Joe, they *really* added up.)

Jane

Jane's one-day net Calorie consumption was over 3200 Calories. With an activity adjusted BMR of about 2040, Jane took in over fifty percent more Calories than her body needed. If her Calorie consumption and activity level remain the same throughout the week of her trip, she can expect to arrive home a couple of pounds heavier than when she left.

A closer look at Jane's logs reveal where these extra Calories came from. Jane ate more servings from the junk food group than from all the other food groups together! Combine that eating habit with very little exercise and it is a recipe for weight gain.

Mary

Mary did a great job of balancing her Calories across food groups as well as spreading them out over the course of the day. She made some very good choices in the foods she ate and put in some time exercising. She ended the day slightly under her daily net Calorie goal.

Mary has a great start realizing her ultimate body weight goal. She should see some results by the time she gets back home, and her success at achieving her daily net Calorie goal should give her the motivation to continue.

MODEL PLANS

Joe

Joe consumed over 4400 Calories and burned off fewer than 100 excess Calories with a couple of short walks for a net daily Calorie total of 4380. For the sedentary lifestyle that Joe is adopting for his vacation, his activity adjusted BMR is around 2360. So on this particular day he took in an excess of over 2000 Calories. If he does this each day of his two week trip, he can expect to pack on an additional eight pounds or so by the time he returns home.

A closer look at Joe's logs reveal from where those extra Calories came. Joe had almost as many servings from the junk food group as the rest of the food groups combined. Even when he made good food choices such as a salad or a potato, he added dressing or a topping that more than doubled the number of Calories eaten. And, of course, it didn't help that he got almost no exercise.

Max

Max did a great job of following THE COMPLETE TRAVEL DIET. He consumed around 2000 Calories and burned off nearly 400 of them with some brisk walks. He achieved his daily net Calorie goal and then some. He did a fair job of balancing his diet to attain the recommended servings of each of the food groups, and he was able to satisfactorily spread his Caloric intake over the day.

By reviewing his daily Calorie log, Max will be able to make some minor adjustments to better distribute his food group servings over the following days and should have little problem meeting his two-week, as well as his longer term, body weight goal.

THE COMPLETE TRAVEL DIET

Lessons learned

What general lessons can we learn from reviewing the Calorie logs of our hypothetical travelers? Here are a few that stand out.

The Calorie logs are inaccurate—but useful

Often there is a significant difference between the actual Calories in a meal and the estimate of those Calories made by simply logging the servings. There will always be some discrepancy between actual and estimated daily Calories, though the differences tend to diminish over a period of a day or two.

For example, reviewing Mary's logs and using values derived from the USDA's National Nutrient Database (those are the numbers in brackets next to the food items), we find a four percent difference between her actual and her estimated daily Calorie consumption. Smaller differences in the figures are found for Jane, Joe, and Max. This is normal and expected because THE COMPLETE TRAVEL DIET favors simplicity over accuracy. In fact it makes a point of it.

Moreover, though daily Calorie logs provide a moderately accurate picture of Calories consumed and burned, their real value lies in the process of recording each food item eaten and each activity completed. Through this process, you are constantly reminded of how the daily choices about what you eat and how you move affect your weight.

Small shifts can make big differences

If Joe had chosen to eat an apple and drink a diet soda instead of the potato chips and regular cola he had as an afternoon snack, he would have cut over 400 Calories from his diet—almost as many Calories as he would burn if he were to walk briskly for an hour.

By the same token, if Jane had put in 35 minutes of brisk walking, she would have doubled the excess Calories she burned and would have come five percent closer to her activity adjusted BMR.

Small behavioral changes can, over time, make big differences.

Junk food can sink a diet

It bears mentioning again how much influence the selections from the junk food group affected the total number of Calories consumed by Jane and Joe. About one-third of their Calorie consumption came from this Calorie-rich, nutrition-poor, but very tasty food group.

Like Jane and Joe, the diets of many travelers get derailed by the opportunities that travel provides to eat poorly. Don't be one of them.

Moderate exercise counts

Mary was able to pare 400 Calories from her daily Calorie consumption by spending an extra 45 minutes walking and jogging. Max was able to burn almost that many Calories off his daily Calorie consumption by doing nothing more strenuous than walking for about an hour.

For vegetarians

If you are a vegetarian, you are probably adept at finding a variety of nutritional sources where others may not look. This can give you an advantage over others when facing the challenges of healthful eating while traveling.

Because fruits and vegetables are the primary source of nutrients in your diet, you must eat a variety of plant foods to get enough protein as well as proper amounts of the vitamins

THE COMPLETE TRAVEL DIET

and minerals that typically come from animal sources in non-vegetarian diets—specifically vitamin D, vitamin B12, iron, calcium, and zinc. (This can be even trickier if you adopt a vegan diet. Under this stricter vegetarian diet, you are allowed no animal foods such as eggs or dairy products.)

Here are alternative sources of protein, vitamins, and minerals.

- **Protein** - plant foods such as lentils, tofu, nuts, seeds, tempeh, miso, and peas.

- **Vitamin D** - fortified milk (including soymilk), cereals, and sunlight.

- **Vitamin B12** - fortified milk, cereals, eggs, and foods made from soybeans such as tempeh, miso, and soymilk.

- **Iron** - rice, lentils, cashews, tofu, tomato juice, and garbanzo beans.

- **Calcium** - fortified dairy products, fortified orange juice, tofu, and broccoli.

- **Zinc** - whole grains, dairy products, nuts, tofu, leafy vegetables such as spinach, and root vegetables such as carrots.

NINE

Travel tips

Applying what you know about diet, exercise, and attitude.

In this chapter, you will find 170 tips to help you reach your goal of maintaining your weight or losing a few pounds while traveling.

Don't use all these tips. That would be too much to ask and too difficult to implement. Instead, choose one or two tips to incorporate into your routine as you begin your travels. If those serve you well, then add in a few more until you find the right mix of advice that works best for you.

Not all the tips are applicable to you or to all traveling situations. Implement the advice you find of value and simply ignore the rest. And don't hesitate to discontinue following any advice that doesn't work for you.

Finally, the tips offered in this chapter are cumulative. For instance, the advice to keep yourself hydrated (*Tip #53*) is only found in the first section on transportation, but this advice is important and applicable wherever you travel.

Safety and security

Your safety and security while traveling should be paramount. While most of the tips provided here require only a simple change in your traveling behavior, don't let your enthusiasm for losing weight displace your common sense.

Sanitation practices during food preparation can be uncertain—particularly in developing countries where regulations and monitoring is sketchy. Even in some of the finest restaurants, sanitary conditions can be compromised. It doesn't hurt to take a quick look in the kitchen on the way to your table to see that everything appears clean. And you should absolutely think twice before ordering up a daily special from in a walkup restaurant.

Also, travelers are often prime targets of criminals who see them as vulnerable sources of revenue. So exercise caution when, for instance, venturing into neighborhoods near your hotel for an evening walk.

Before you go

When you prepare for a trip, you probably consider such things as how long you will be away, the predicted weather at your destination, and the activities in which you will get involved. You then pack the clothes you'll wear and sundries you'll use while on your trip. Now extend this thinking to controlling your weight.

Will you be in one place long enough to develop an eating or exercise routine? Will the weather at your destination allow you to exercise outdoors? Will you need rainwear while walking or jogging? Will the activities you have planned make it easy to find healthy foods and contribute to you getting exercise?

When you plan, plan with weight control in mind.

Plan your diet

Tip #1 Eat

I want to make these tips welcome and easily followed, not dreadful and complicated. So right off the bat, I'm offering up a piece of advice that dieters often overlook. You will not be successful in the long run if you don't eat well and eat regularly during your trip.

Make sure you have at least three healthful meals each day whether in transit or at your destination. (Smaller meals eaten more often are even better if you can arrange it.) This will provide you with the Calories you need and will prevent the occurrence of food cravings that you might otherwise experience if you skip a meal.

You probably plan when you will visit a monument or meet with a client, but do you plan when and where you will eat your meals? You should because eating modest, healthful meals on a regular schedule is the key to weight control when traveling.

When planning your trip, plan your meals—not only what you will eat, but also when you will eat it. Establishing an eating schedule will help you regulate your intake of Calories throughout the day, and if you have

THE COMPLETE TRAVEL DIET

an inclination to skip or delay your meals, scheduling mealtimes will help to avoid the consequent tendency to overeat later.

Also, just as certain tourist attractions close to the public during certain periods of the day and business associates become unavailable for appointments, set time periods when you will not eat (e.g., one hour prior to retiring for the evening).

Tip #2 *Modify social engagements*
If you have plans to dine at restaurants known for less than healthful foods or larger than appropriate portions, change or cancel those plans before departing on your trip. If you can't, decide now what food items you will order and how you will control portion size.

Tip #3 *Identify heart-healthy restaurants*
Do the advance work to find restaurants at your destination(s) that offer American Heart Association heart-healthy menu items. (Try searching the Internet for "heart-healthy restaurants <city name>".) Heart-healthy dishes are generally lower in fat and Calories than similar items on the menu.

Tip #4 *Pack a snack*
You pack shoes, underwear, and toothpaste. Now consider packing whole grains and/or low-fat foods as well. It is far better to know that you are carrying healthful snacks that you can consume on your own timetable than to rely on others to supply foods of unknown Caloric content delivered on an irregular schedule. It takes very little planning to provide yourself with snacks that are more healthful than you can find aboard airplanes or trains.

TRAVEL TIPS

Tip #5 Take a shake
Instead of skipping a meal, replace it with a shake and a piece of fruit. You'll save yourself money, time, and at least 150 Calories. Just remember that replacement shakes should not be substituted for all your meals. Try to limit their use.

Tip #6 Take fresh fruit...
Fruits often come in their own containers. Apples, oranges, and bananas, for instance, are packaged by nature and ready to transport. And because fresh fruits contain both simple and complex carbohydrates, they are the ideal food for an immediate pick-me-up as well as providing energy over the longer term.

Tip #7 ...or dried fruit
If fresh fruits are unavailable, cannot be adequately protected during travel, are banned from transporting, or are just too inconvenient to carry, substitute dried fruits that avoid these shortcomings. Beware, however, that some dried fruits are processed with additional sugar.

Tip #8 Carry water
Because you can never be assured that drinking water will be available, carry enough of it for your needs until you are sure more will be obtainable.

Tip #9 Cart a cooler
If you are driving from home, carting along a cooler in the trunk of your car should be a given. You'll be able to buy and transport more healthful food than you will likely be able to purchase along the way in roadside restaurants. You can generally get ice for a cooler from your hotel, in markets, or in service stations.

If you are not driving to your destination but will be using a rental car for an extended period while you are

THE COMPLETE TRAVEL DIET

there, you may be able to buy a cooler when you arrive. (Styrofoam coolers are cheap and can be left behind when you depart.) Or you can take along a hard-sided, plastic cooler that can even be used as a suitcase while you are in transit.

Plan your activities

Tip #10 Plan for an active trip

Watching others participate does little to help you lose or maintain your weight while on the road. Don't just be an onlooker to the activities of others. Rather than planning to sit on a beach, make a reservation to take a surfing lesson. Instead of preparing to look out over a lake, contact a local outfitter to reserve a canoe. Instead of anticipating sitting on your veranda taking in the mountain scenery, pack your hiking boots. Call your hotel or a local sporting goods retailer to find out what's happening so that you can get involved.

Tip #11 Schedule time for exercise

Plan *at least* 30 minutes of exercise every day. Just as you must schedule an airline flight or make reservations at popular restaurants, schedule your physical activities to achieve this minimum level of exercise.

How can you get in a half hour every day when you are traveling? It's easy because the 30 minutes does not have to come all at the same time. Your exercise can be taken in five- to ten-minute chunks. (There are advantages to continuous exercise lasting 30 minutes or longer, but for weight loss or maintenance, a cumulative 30 minutes is fine.)

If you know, for instance, that you have an hour between connecting flights, use some of that time to walk up and down the concourse. If you have an hour

TRAVEL TIPS

between appointments, perhaps you can walk between them. However you can get your time in,

Tip #12   *Schedule a lesson*
Want to improve your golf game? Sign up for a lesson at a local golf course.

Want to learn how to play tennis? Get to a local park for a class.

Interested in Tai Chi? Check the local telephone book for schools and instructors.

Tip #13   *Meet for a walk instead of a meal*
There is nothing magic about meeting for lunch or dinner. Indeed, there may be more magic in meeting for a walk where your mind can be on the topic of the meeting rather than on food.

Tip #14   *Do the legwork when reserving accommodations*
Do the advance legwork to find a hotel that provides guest access to a good health club or offers an in-room fitness program.

Tip #15   *Book a health-friendly hotel*
If you stay in a hotel that emphasizes its health programs, chances are the facilities will be well maintained, and there will be a variety of activities from which to choose. It is also more probable that the on-site restaurants will offer more healthful meal choices.

Tip #16   *Find exercise facilities*
Though a formal gym or exercise facility is not necessary for you to get in your daily activity, it may be more convenient, more motivating, and/or safer if a health club or fitness facility is available at your hotel. All other things being equal, choose a hotel with an on-site gym.

THE COMPLETE TRAVEL DIET

Tip #17 Select an accessible seat
   If given a choice when booking your transportation, reserve an aisle seat so you can get up often and move around.

Tip #18 Prepare for in-transit exercise
   If there are opportunities to exercise while in-transit (see *Tip #59*), pack your exercise gear in your carry-on luggage.

Tip #19 Pack comfortable clothes first
   The first clothes to go into your suitcase should be the ones that you will use to exercise. If you run out of room in your luggage, remove other clothes. Keep your exercise gear in there!

Tip #20 Pack an exercise video
   When you make lodging reservations request rooms with VCRs or DVD players and take along your favorite workout tape or disc.

Tip #21 Pack comfortable shoes
   A very effective, Calorie-burning exercise is simply walking—an activity that is easy to take part in while traveling. Make sure that a pair of sturdy and comfortable shoes is among your clothes.

Tip #22 Lose the rollers
   Use luggage without wheels. The more weight you carry, the more Calories you will burn—whether it's packed under your belt or strapped over your shoulder.

Tip #23 Travel on foot
   If you are a leisure traveler, choose activities that require you to move in the course of enjoying them. Sign up for walking tours or short hikes. Walk

through museums and art galleries. And avoid shortcuts—take the long way 'round.

If you are traveling on business, walk to and from your meetings whenever possible. Walk during the breaks as well.

Tip #24 Conduct your affairs while on the move
If you take meetings during your travels, take them on the move rather than sitting and snacking. Hold a "business walk" in lieu of a sit-down meeting.

Tip #25 Use exercise as a pick-me-up
While others may find energy in sweets, fats, or caffeine, use moderate exercise to refresh and reinvigorate yourself.

Tip #26 Link daily physical activity to your itinerary
If you plan to read a newspaper every day, for instance, plan to exercise while riding a stationary bicycle. Or if you watch or listen to a particular television or radio program, do it while exercising.

Tip #27 Get a pedometer and use it
Using time to estimate the Calories burned while exercising is generally sufficient for travelers. However, if you want a more accurate record of the distance you travel, a pedometer is a good investment. Moreover, keeping records of your time and distance can be a good motivator to help you keep up the activity.

Plan your attitude

Tip #28 Pack your daily logs
Because keeping daily records of the foods you eat and the exercises you complete is one of the most important things you can do to ensure success in reaching your weight loss goal, you *must* carry your logs and keep them current.

THE COMPLETE TRAVEL DIET

Losing weight requires discipline, and completing entries into your logs after every meal and every activity helps you maintain that discipline.

Tip #29 *Pack your daily logs*
(Keeping daily food and activity logs is so important to losing weight that it needed repeating.)

Tip #30 *Psyche yourself down*
Before every meal, pause for a moment to review your daily food log. Look over the food selections you have made so far during the day and the daily Calorie goal you set for yourself. Note the distribution of marks across the food group columns and plan your meal accordingly.

Tip #31 *Eliminate travel-related food culprits*
Many people eat some high-Calorie foods while traveling that they would usually avoid while in their home environment. Identify foods—especially high-Calorie foods—that you eat while traveling that you would rarely eat at any other times. (For me it's Corn Nuts®.)

Be as specific as you can. For instance, don't just plan to eliminate "snacks." Instead plan to eliminate "airline peanuts." (By the way, if you take a dozen flights a year where you are offered but you refuse a ½-ounce bag of peanuts on each flight, you would eliminate about 1000 Calories a year from your diet.)

Tip #32 *Don't eat what you hate*
Don't force yourself to eat foods you don't like simply because they are deemed "healthful." (Lima beans are a good source of fiber, B vitamins, magnesium, potassium, and phytochemicals, and are low in Calories. Nevertheless, you'll never find them on my plate—I can't stand them.)

TRAVEL TIPS

Tip #33 Leave something on your plate
You have my permission... no, you have my encouragement to leave food on your plate. Stop eating when you have consumed an appropriate number of rightly-sized portions of foods from a variety of food groups. Don't eat just because food is available. You should never leave a meal feeling stuffed.

Tip #34 Try a new food every day or two
If you're bored with what you're eating, you're likely to cheat. Or worse, you may abandon your diet altogether. Trying out new foods will give you the opportunity to concentrate on their unique tastes and textures rather than focusing on their fat or Calorie content. A real benefit of travel is the variety of foods from which you can choose.

Tip #35 Take "comfort walks"
When you travel, you will be exposed to the hassles and the crowding associated with travel. These are known contributors to stress. In your search for relief from that stress, you may turn to food—"comfort food" some call it. Recognizing this common behavior is the first step in short-circuiting the connection between stress brought on by travel and eating in response to it.

Once you realize that you may be seeking food in response to stress rather than to hunger, you can use other ways to manage that stress. Physical activity, in particular, cannot only alleviate stress, it can have a longer lasting effect than does eating. And the change of scenery that usually accompanies a walk or a jog can add to the beneficial effect of the exercise.

You may still take comfort in those foods that make you feel better, but portion control is very important—a handful of chips rather than a whole bag, a

The Complete Travel Diet

scoop of ice cream in a bowl instead of a double scoop in a cone with sprinkles. Or substitute foods such as popcorn (hold the butter) instead of potato chips; ginger snaps instead of chocolate-chip cookies.

Tip #36 Avoid scales
The inaccuracies of common scales and the variabilities among them are substantial. Determining a true fraction of a pound difference in your weight from one day to the next is nearly impossible while traveling. Weigh yourself on your scale before you leave on your trip if you like, and weigh yourself on the same scale when you return. But don't weigh yourself during the interim.

Tip #37 Take things to do with your mind
Some people eat simply because they are bored. An occupied mind does not dwell on the next meal so pack plenty of interesting things to do.

Tip #38 Play games
A crossword puzzle or a game of cards will occupy your mind and keep it off of food. Just make sure that you don't "accessorize" your playing area with fatty snacks.

Tip #39 Read
Involvement in a good book can take your mind off many things—including food. (Hint: Don't make it a cookbook.)

Tip #40 Replace a fork with a pen
Write a letter to a friend, make a list of gifts to purchase, or just jot down some "to-do" notes to yourself. This will keep both your hands and your mind occupied.

TRAVEL TIPS

Tip #41 Travel with a "believer"
If you have the opportunity, travel with another person who has already adopted a lifestyle that is compatible with the principles outlined in THE COMPLETE TRAVEL DIET.

Tip #42 Travel with a recruit
Alternately, travel with someone who, like you, is trying to make some lifestyle changes and who could benefit from some of the recommendations of THE COMPLETE TRAVEL DIET.

Tip #43 Pack a list of goals
Just as you may make a list of the goals you hope to accomplish while traveling on business or the sites you want to see while touring, prepare an outline of the plan you intend to follow while traveling and tape or pin it to the top of your suitcase.

Tip #44 Pack motivational slips
For each day that you will be gone, place a slip of paper with a motivational helper in each set of underwear you will wear while away.

Tip #45 Stand clear of food
If you are at a social event that includes hors d'oeuvres or buffet tables, locate yourself away from the food so that you won't be tempted to "graze."

Set a "social goal" for yourself to take your mind off of the food. If you are traveling on business, try to make a business contact. If you are on vacation, try to make a new friend. Or join in any activity that may accompany the event—except the pie-eating contest, of course.

THE COMPLETE TRAVEL DIET

Tip #46 Get your sleep
Sleep deprivation and fatigue can lead to a loss of energy, which in turn can lead to food cravings—especially cravings for sugary foods. Getting plenty of rest and catching up on lost sleep will help prevent these physiologically induced cravings.

Plan your return

Tip #47 "Unpack" your kitchen
You won't want to come home to a freezer full of ice cream or a pantry stocked up with chips following a trip where you were able to maintain your weight or even lose weight. Get rid of high-Calorie, low-nutrition foods before you leave on your trip.

Tip #48 Make a shopping list
When you return from your travels, you will probably have to restock your pantry and refrigerator. Make a list of foods to purchase upon your return so that you will be able to continue a healthy diet.

Tip #49 Set up an exercise routine
Set up a home-based exercise schedule before you leave. It may have to be modified upon your return, but something will be in place so that you can easily continue your exercise routine.

Tip #50 Disable your TV's remote control
A remote control device for your TV allows you to sit for hours without ever having to move from your favorite chair. Make the remote control unavailable before you leave home. You will have to move to change channels.

Transportation

Today's traveler is likely to be transported by airplane and/or train. While travel aboard a modern airliner or high-speed train can be confining and the food options available rather narrow, it doesn't have to disrupt your eating or exercise plan.

Airports, train stations, and the like usually offer a number of places to eat. Unfortunately having a variety of establishments available does not translate into having a variety of healthful foods from which to choose. Indeed much of the food served in transportation terminals is processed, preserved, and packaged with quick delivery, rather than nutritional value, in mind.

Diet

Tip #51 Order a low-Calorie meal...
Most airlines and some passenger service trains allow you to order a low-Calorie meal. However, you must order it at least 24 hours in advance.

Tip #52 ... or pack your own
Transportation terminals offer convenient and therefore tempting places to eat while in transit. But that convenience can come at a price when trying to adhere to a low-Calorie diet. Instead of hoping that you may find something on the menu in a terminal restaurant, bring along your own food so that you know exactly what you will be eating and in what portion size.

You can use a simple insulated lunch bag packed with a sandwich, some vegetables and fruit. Put ice in a sealed bag to keep it cold. When you finish your meal, you can discard the ice and fold up the bag for your return trip.

THE COMPLETE TRAVEL DIET

Tip #53 *Stay hydrated*
You should be aware of the possibility of dehydration while in-transit. The humidity level on a commercial aircraft is often lower than that found in a desert. Dehydration interferes with your body's ability to metabolize stored fat and your kidneys' ability to flush out waste.

Keeping yourself well hydrated will not only facilitate the functioning of your body, it is one of the best defenses against food cravings. It can suppress your appetite by giving you a feeling of fullness. Water is fundamental to the success of any diet plan, but remember that you have to drink it, not just carry it.

Tip #54 *Limit caffeine and alcohol*
Alcohol and to a lesser extent caffeine can act as diuretics—not the effect you are looking for when you are trying to keep yourself hydrated.

Tip #55 *Drink on command*
Think of a trigger word or event and every time that word or event comes up, drink. For instance, whenever a pilot makes an announcement, drink; or take a couple swallows every quarter hour.

Tip #56 *Plan restroom breaks*
If you are drinking the amount of water suggested, you will find it necessary to urinate more often than you are probably used to now.

Tip #57 *Every time you pee, drink*
In order to stay hydrated, you must keep replenishing the liquids in your system.

TRAVEL TIPS

Activity

Tip #58 *"Move" in the passenger compartment*
Pay attention to staying flexible and maintaining good circulation while sitting for long periods. Regularly stretch your legs and do in-seat exercises. Better yet, get out of your seat and walk. Try to get at least five minutes of exercise for every hour in transit.

Tip #59 *Use a gym between connections*
Some major airports and train stations have on-site gyms or provide access to nearby health clubs that you can visit on a transient basis, and some transportation terminals have shower facilities. If you are motivated and know that you have an extended time to wait between connections, you may be able to change into exercise gear, use the facilities, and freshen up before returning to your travels. (An online listing of gyms that are in or near airports is available at www.airportgyms.com.)

Tip #60 *Use terminals as gyms*
While transportation terminals may not be the best places to find low-Calorie, nutritional fare, they can be wonderful places to burn Calories. There are long stretches to walk and stairs to climb. Terminals are large, typically air conditioned, and relatively secure.

Tip #61 *Walk*
Whenever possible, avoid using trams, moving sidewalks, people movers, escalators, elevators, or other mechanical conveyances. Walking between gates at a large airport can easily take 10 minutes, and if you are carrying luggage, you get an extra workout. You can easily burn 50 Calories just making connecting flights.

THE COMPLETE TRAVEL DIET

Tip #62 Disembark one stop early
　　When traveling by light rail or bus or even taxi, get off at a stop prior to your destination then walk the rest of the way. (Doing this when traveling by air is a little too ambitious.)

Tip #63 Use a distant convenience
　　Walk to restrooms or telephones or water coolers that are *not* located nearby. With a brisk, five-minute walk to a restroom and a five-minute walk back, you'll have completed a third of a modest daily exercise routine.

Tip #64 Say "no" to on-board snacks
　　Feed yourself from your own "stash" of healthful snacks rather than the high-Calorie snacks that you are likely to be offered on commercial airliners or available on trains. And water should almost always be selected over other beverages.

Tip #65 Walk while using a mobile phone
　　An advantage of carrying a mobile telephone when you travel is that… well, it is mobile. And the advantage of using it while you are traveling is that you too can be moving. So while on the telephone, get in some walking.

Lodging

　　The primary business of the lodging industry is to provide safe, clean, quiet accommodations for those who are away from home. As an added source of revenue to these establishments and as a benefit to their guests, many hotels, motels and other lodging businesses include restaurant or cafeteria services. With a few exceptions, however, the focus of these businesses is on the housing of their guests and only secondarily on the feeding of them. Consequently, many hotel restaurants and motel cafeterias—not all, but many—serve an abundance of processed foods. The upshot of this for you as a conscientious dieter is to be extra selective when dining "on property."

Diet

Tip #66 Book a suite with a kitchenette
If you have a facility available to prepare your own meals, you can make what you want and control portion sizes. Moreover, you will be less likely to skip breakfast.

Tip #67 Get a distant room
Ask for a room farthest from the lobby, the pool, the spa, and definitely farthest from the restaurant. The farther you have to walk, the more Calories you will burn getting to and from your room.

Tip #68 Use the mini-bar…
If your room is equipped with a small refrigerator, use it to store wholesome snacks and drinks that you bring with you or extra portions of an oversized meal that you got from a restaurant.

Tip #69 …but not its contents
The food and beverage items that are stocked in hotel room mini-bars are typically high in fat—not to mention outrageously priced.

Tip #70 Leave the bathroom light on
If you are drinking water to the extent recommended, you will be up at least once in the night to pee. If not, the light burning in the morning will remind you to increase your water consumption.

THE COMPLETE TRAVEL DIET

Activity

Tip #71 Don't use valet parking
Ever wonder why parking valets look so trim? Well, while you are standing in wait for your car, a valet is running off to retrieve it. Be your own valet. You'll burn a few Calories and save a few bucks to boot.

Tip #72 Park in the farthest parking spot
Park your car at the end of the parking lot or in the next lot over. Better yet, park down the street and hoof it back to your hotel. The extra few minutes will add up. And if you are carrying luggage, your Calorie burn rate will be even higher.

Tip #73 Use stairs instead of elevators or escalators
Lifting your body weight as well as moving it forward is a great Calorie burner. You get both benefits when climbing stairs, and the time on the stairs counts toward your daily total of activity minutes.

Tip #74 Carry your bags to your room
For every 25 pounds you carry 100 yards, you burn an additional 8½ Calories—not a lot, but like every other movement you make, it adds up.

Tip #75 Unpack your exercise clothes
You want them in sight. You want them to call to you, to make you feel like you have to use them.

Tip #76 Find the gym
Soon after check-in, visit the exercise facility in your hotel to prepare yourself for its use and to give you a little motivational spike.

If you are staying at an establishment with no facilities, ask if your hotel maintains an association with a nearby health club that you can use for free or at a

TRAVEL TIPS

discount. You can also search for clubs near your hotel at www.healthclubs.com.

Tip #77 *Do your own bidding*
From valet parking to turndown service, hotels court their customers by providing services so that their guests have to do the least exertion possible. In your case, that runs counter to your objective of getting the most exercise as possible. If you need something from the hotel, get it yourself.

Tip #78 *Don't use room service*
If you want to eat in your room, walk to the restaurant to order a take-out meal.

Tip #79 *Start your day on the move*
Get up 30 minutes earlier in the morning, and take a brisk walk to start your day.

Tip #80 *Enlist a companion*
Need someone to get you going? Schedule your walk or exercise routine with a traveling companion or colleague.

Tip #81 *Use the exercise equipment at your destination*
Large hotels often have elaborate gym arrangements, and even the smallest boutique hotels put in treadmills or stationary bicycles.

Tip #82 *Get ready to exercise*
The hardest part of exercising is often putting on your gym garb and sticking your foot out of your hotel room door. Once you're suited up and headed toward the gym, you will have begun a process that is likely to carry you through.

Tip #83 *Don't turn on the TV in your room*
Get out and walk. Go get a magazine or a newspaper or a book. Or just get out and sightsee.

The Complete Travel Diet

Tip #84   Listen to the news
Instead of watching news on the television, carry a wearable radio, and listen to the news while you walk.

Tip #85   Leave the remote near the TV
If you choose to watch television, at least get up and move to the TV when you want to change the channel.

Tip #86   Rent an exercise video instead of a movie
If you have a choice of videos from your hotel's video programming or if there is a video cassette player in your hotel room, select an exercise video and put in a half hour's activity in your hotel room. (Not too much stomping, please.) Or better yet, rent an exercise video *and* a movie. You can watch the movie while you cool down and it can be the reward following the activity.

Restaurants

Compared to the costs of labor, facilities, management, and administration, food is not particularly expensive for restaurants. So restaurants often compete by increasing the number of items included on their menus or by increasing the sizes of the portions served or both. Indeed, many restaurants have increased the size of their dinner plates from 10 to 12 inches. Consequently it is especially important to select menu items with care and exercise portion control when dining out.

There are many tips for taking meals in restaurants. Before getting to those tips, however, consider not eating in a restaurant at all.

Restaurant alternative

Tip #87   Shop for yourself
An alternative to eating in restaurants is to avoid them altogether by shopping at a grocery store for your

TRAVEL TIPS

meal. With very little effort and in much less time than it can take in all but fast-food restaurants, you will be able to purchase healthful food items that are ready to eat.

Tip #88 *Make a grocery list*
When you go shopping at a grocery store, make a list to keep you on track. That way you are more likely to purchase healthful foods than foods that are distributed by companies that have paid placement fees to have their products positioned in front of you.

Tip #89 *Shop the edges*
In general, you will likely find more healthful foods in the peripheral aisles of a grocery store. As you wander into the inner aisles, you are more likely to encounter high-Calorie foods.

Tip #90 *Buy small*
Most grocery stores aren't set up to cater to travelers looking to purchase just enough food for a single meal. It is easy to buy too much food. On the other hand, many of the food items that are the most healthful (fresh fruits and vegetables, for instance) are usually carried in bulk so that you can easily select one or two items.

Tip #91 *Select single servings*
When shopping in a local market, choose foods packaged in individual serving sizes to prevent overeating. Remember, however, that the portions allocated as "single serving" may be considerably greater than the portions called for in THE COMPLETE TRAVEL DIET.

Tip #92 *Avoid eating eat out of a bag or box*
It is difficult enough to mete out correct portion sizes from the various food groups. Trying to allocate them without seeing the whole portion at once is even more

difficult, and often leads to over apportionment. Before you begin to consume a food, place single portions on your plate or in a bowl. That way you will be able to more correctly judge how much you are eating.

If you choose to take your meals in restaurants, the following general tips will help you stay on your plan.

Diet

Tip #93 First drink water
Drink a glass of water before beginning your meal. This will aid in the digestive process, and give your stomach a certain sense of fullness.

Tip #94 Don't drink your servings
Try not to spend your Calorie allotment on sugary drinks such as sodas or shakes. Choose instead skim milk, tea, coffee, or plain water. You'll have more of a sense of fullness if you eat than if you consume the same number of Calories by drinking high-Calorie beverages.

Tip #95 Avoid alcohol
Wait until after your meal to enjoy an alcoholic beverage so that the alcohol will not interfere with your ability and resolve to maintain good eating habits.

If you feel as though you need to "appear" to be drinking alcohol—I'm not sure why that would be—simply sip tonic or soda water.

Tip #96 Take your coffee or tea black
If you drink coffee or tea, don't add natural or artificial sweeteners. And avoid "whiteners." Think of them instead as "fatteners."

TRAVEL TIPS

Tip #97 *Eat slowly*
It can take a while for your stomach to signal your brain that it is satisfied. By slowing down the pace of eating, you give your brain a chance to catch up with how your body feels, and you also become more aware of how much food you're eating.

Tip #98 *Eat dessert ...*
Don't deprive yourself, but do make intelligent choices. Choose fruit over sweets for dessert. You *can* have ice cream for dessert, but you may have to pass on the salad dressing or the potato topping that you might otherwise have ordered with your meal.

Tip #99 *... or just whiff the dessert tray*
There is some evidence that the odor of sweet desserts has a satiating effect on the craving for sweets. Of course, the sight of a dessert may also stimulate a craving, so if you choose this technique, take a whiff, and quickly get the dessert out of sight. And if you find that the aroma of sweet desserts increases your desire for them, mark this bit of advice off your list of tips right now.

Tip #100 *Go for fresh fruit*
Having recommended that you should satisfy your desire for desserts by smelling them instead of tasting them, now let's "get real." When you do choose to have dessert, and you can, select naturally sweet foods like fruits rather than foods that contain added sugars such as cake or pie.

Tip #101 *Eat "alone"*
Don't eat while involved in other activities like watching television, reading a newspaper, or responding to emails. These other activities are distracters that make you less likely to be aware of what you are eating. If you snack while involved in other

activities, portion out the snack ahead of time rather than eating from its container so that you will be less likely to overeat.

Activity

Tip #102 Walk to a nearby restaurant
Whenever possible, walk to and from restaurants. A ten minute walk to and from a restaurant can burn up a few hundred Calories.

Tip #103 Walk instead of waiting in the bar
If the wait for a table at a restaurant will be more than 10 minutes, take a short walk instead of bellying up to the bar. You will be contributing to your daily physical activity while avoiding the extra Calories in alcohol.

Tip #104 Get it to-go...
Instead of taking your coffee or tea at your table following your meal, get it to go (ask for a "go cup") and take it—and yourself—for a walk.

Tip #105 ...or go get it
Walk to another restaurant, coffee shop, or lounge for a healthful desert or an after-meal beverage.

Restaurant style

When traveling, there is a very good chance that you will take many, if not most or all of your meals in restaurants. The benefit of this is that you are generally offered a wide variety of foods from which to choose, and it minimizes the time you are around food. The drawback is that you must rely on others to select and prepare the foods you eat.

NOTE: While the previous tips relate to eating in almost any restaurant, the following tips seem to be more applicable to particular restaurant styles—fast-food, casual dining, or fine dining—and that is how they have been assigned. Nevertheless, many of the tips included under one style apply to other dining situations as well.

Fast-food dining

Fast-food restaurants are just that: Fast. The emphasis is on speed of delivery rather than ambiance, presentation, or too often, health. Chances are that you will be drawn to one of these restaurants if your travel schedule requires a "quick" meal. Though there is a vast opportunity to make poor decisions about your food choices, fast-foods can, with a little bit of know-how, be part of a healthy weight loss program.

Though these types of establishments are not typically known for low-fat fare or the ease with which you can get specially prepared meals, there is much you can do to guard against eating the high-fat, high-Calorie meals that often define these establishments.

Restaurant selection

Tip #106 Choose a deli or sandwich shop
You are likely to find more healthful, quickly-delivered meals in a delicatessen or sandwich shop than in a typical fast-food restaurant, especially one that promotes fried food.

Food selection

Tip #107 Rehearse your order
Millions of dollars are spent on medial and in-store advertising and promotions to get you to order what restaurants want you to order, not what may be best for you. Before you step inside a restaurant, know what you are going to order and resist offers to "up-grade" and especially to "up-size" your order. Though it may not be easy, look past the eye-catching photos and add-on "deals."

THE COMPLETE TRAVEL DIET

Tip #108 Lower the fat
Select lower fat meat alternatives such as turkey or chicken rather than high-fat, processed meats such as sausages, salami, bologna, liverwurst or other cold cuts.

Tip #109 Substitute for meat
Replace meat with vegetable products such as vegetable burger patties or soy-based foodstuffs.

Tip #110 Add vegetables
Add lettuce, tomato, onion, sprouts, cucumber, peppers, or other vegetable garnishes to your sandwich to get a share of your daily vegetable food group servings and some fiber.

Tip #111 Moderate the carbohydrates
Ask that your sandwich be served on a whole-wheat roll or multi-grain bun. You can further lower the Calories by asking that the inner, doughy part of the roll be removed.

Tip #112 Order plain
An otherwise low-Calorie sandwich can turn into a high-Calorie meal by the addition of mayonnaise, ketchup, relish, barbeque sauce, and other condiments. To best control for the Calories that are piled on to a sandwich by the addition of high-Calorie sauces, order your sandwich "plain" and plop on your own reduced-Calorie condiments if you like (see *Tip #115*).

Tip #113 Avoid "fried"...
If you choose a cooked meal, keep in mind that almost any other means of heat preparation is better than frying, which can easily double the Calories of the food. Order your meal grilled, baked, steamed,

poached, roasted, broiled, stir-fried, or even microwaved. But not simply fried.

Tip #114 ... and sauce-based preparations...
Foods that are sautéed or baked in casseroles do not allow fat to escape. Foods served with heavy sauces or gravies, can add more Calories back in than might have been cooked out

Tip #115 ... and really avoid "deep-fried"
Deep-fried foods have *excessive* amounts of fat and Calories.

Meal management

Tip #116 Add your own dressing
To make sure you get the dressing you want and in the quantities that you want it, bring your own. Many food companies offer their dressings in convenient, individual serving packets, often in reduced-fat varieties, and are available through restaurant supply stores.

Tip #117 Eat sweets last
Save your consumption of sweets for after-meal treats when there is fiber in your digestive system to slow the absorption of glucose.

Casual dining

Casual dining restaurants generally have a more leisurely atmosphere, are more comfortable, and usually have a more extensive menu than fast-food restaurants. Nevertheless, an order in a casual dining restaurant is likely to be prepared following no less of a strict formula than is found in a fast-food eating place so it may require some effort to get the kitchen to prepare an order to meet your request.

THE COMPLETE TRAVEL DIET

Restaurant selection

Tip #118 Avoid odiferous places
If, while you are on the outside of a restaurant, you can smell food being prepared inside, you'd do best to pass it by. The odor you smell is likely from high-fat cooking oil.

Tip #119 Get a table out of the way
Request a table out of the stream of servers who come and go to the kitchen. You are less likely to see and smell the food as it goes by.

Food selection

Tip #120 Don't let the menu drive your order
You should know what you want before you enter a restaurant. Simply order those foods from your server, and let him or her figure out where on the menu those foods are.

Tip #121 Order a la carte
Many entrees come with side dishes that can add Calories to your diet without helping you to fulfill the serving recommendations of the Food Guide Pyramid. Even if you don't think you will eat them, staring at these side dishes can be a temptation you don't need.

By ordering a la carte, you are more likely to get the foods you want, prepared the way you want them rather than a combination of foods chosen by the restaurant for reasons other than your weight loss program.

Tip #122 Split a meal
If an entrée is too much food—many restaurant portions are big enough for two—an alternative to or-

TRAVEL TIPS

dering a la carte is to split a meal with a dining companion. Most restaurants will do this in the kitchen if you ask.

Tip #123 Make an appetizer a meal
With today's generous portion sizes, an appetizer may be a more appropriate sized selection for a main course than a listed entrée.

Tip #124 Order soup
A water-based soup can be nutritious, can be filling, and can supply a portion of your daily water requirement. On the other hand, cream-based soups can be full of fat and should be avoided.

Tip #125 Order a salad
Salads of fresh vegetables with no- or low-fat dressing can be a meal. Combine a salad with soup, and it *is* a meal.

Tip #126 Don't trust "low-fat" options
To appeal to their patrons, restaurants try to deliver the best tasting food they can. Much of the taste of restaurant food, however, comes from fat. Even if you find "low-fat" or "low-Calorie" meals on the menu, they are likely to be higher in fat or Calories than those of packaged foods that carry the same designation.

Although in the United States, the USDA requires that restaurants be able to validate claims that menu items are "low-fat," "low-Calorie," or "light," food preparers may not follow the approved recipes. Moreover, "low-Calorie" is not "no-Calorie." You must still attend to portion size and number of servings.

The Complete Travel Diet

Tip #127 Ask for simple preparation
    Whenever you see the word "oil" or "butter" or "sauce" or "gravy," there is a pretty good bet that you'll find excess Calories. It is almost always prudent to ask your server to omit these in the preparation of your meal.

Tip #128 Order ingredients on the side
    If you want the taste of dressings or sauces, order them on the side so you can control the amount you use when eating.

Tip #129 Add vegetables to your meal
    On a per serving basis, vegetables have the fewest Calories of any of the food groups, and they often supply much of the dietary fiber you need. They are filling, healthful, and low-Calorie. Substitute fresh, raw vegetables for chips or other fried foods that otherwise might be eaten with your meal.

Tip #130 Cut down or eliminate spreads and toppings
    If you want a spread for your bread, request reduced-fat or fat-free margarine instead of butter. Salads and cooked vegetables can be topped with flavored vinegars or lemon juice.

    If you like cream-based toppings for starches such as potatoes or rice, ask for low-fat sour cream, low-fat yogurt, or low-fat cottage cheese. Better yet, because these kinds of substitutions only alter the kinds of fats consumed, not the number of Calories in those fats, steer clear of dairy toppings altogether.

Tip #131 Order with your finger
    If you are unsure that your waiter will understand you (e.g., you are in a foreign country), point to each menu item rather than trying to fake it.

TRAVEL TIPS

Tip #132 Select fresh fruit for dessert
Traditional desserts can easily double the Calorie count of a meal. If you choose to have dessert, select fresh fruit without any added toppings. To splurge, have angel food cake, fat-free frozen yogurt, sherbet, or sorbet. But stay away from ice cream, cake, and pie if and when you can.

Tip #133 Order an extra plate
Knowing in advance that many casual dining restaurants tend to serve too large of portions, request an empty plate to be delivered when your meal is served. If necessary, use the extra plate to down-size your meal to meet the portion sizes you want.

Buffets (a special challenge)

Tip #134 Skip the buffets...
Unless you have extremely strong willpower, pass on any opportunity to serve yourself from a buffet. The availability of high-fat foods, the chance to consume large portions, and a desire to "get your money's worth" may add up to overeating.

Tip #135 ...or at least be selective
If you must serve yourself from a buffet, make a mental list of what foods to gather *before* you head off to the buffet table—and be selective. Choose only the foods on your list and keep the portions small.

Starches and vegetables will be your best bet. At the carving bar, tend toward poultry (without the skin). For dessert, select fresh, not sweetened fruit.

If you are on a cruise, you may find that it is like traveling on a floating buffet. There will be no shortage of food. Indeed, the availability of food almost

THE COMPLETE TRAVEL DIET

anywhere and at any time of day has become the hallmark of cruising. The good news, if there is some, is that much of the food is relatively fresh and healthful. Just be selective.

Meal management

Tip #136 Make sure you get what you ask for...
Some servers may substitute a "reduced-fat" or "low-fat" item when you order "fat-free." To emphasize that you are serious about your fat-free order, put your server on notice by mentioning that, for instance, you could have a severe reaction to fat in your food which could mean a call for medical emergency assistance to be summoned to the restaurant. That should be notice enough.

Tip #137 ... and don't accept what you didn't order
If, for instance, you requested sauce on the side instead of on your food, don't accept your meal if there is sauce glopped on your entrée. Send it back with the server.

Tip #138 Remove the bread... maybe
Unless you order them—and there is no reason you should—request that breads or rolls be removed from your table if they are delivered. If they are made with whole grain, keep the breads or rolls. Just make sure to return any butter or oil that accompany them.

Tip #139 Deny the chips
Even worse than the unrequested delivery of bread made with processed flour is the delivery of a basket of chips to your table—chips that are likely fried in fat. Send them back.

TRAVEL TIPS

Tip #140 Control portion size
When your meal is served, evaluate the portion sizes you have been given. Remove any excess food and place it on an extra plate, then ask your server to remove that plate from the table. ("No," you'll probably say, "The meal is fine. It's just more than I can eat.") This will help prevent you from overeating.

Tip #141 Remove excess fat
Before eating, trim whatever fat is still visible on portions of meat and remove the skin from poultry. This simple maneuver can cut the fat content of a portion by up to one-half.

Tip #142 Distribute dressings and sauces
Instead of pouring dressings or sauces over your food, dip your fork in the dressing or sauce in a side dish before using it to collect bites of food. The dressing or sauce will be more evenly distributed on your food, and you will get a taste with every bite. Better yet, you will use less dressing or sauce than you would otherwise.

Fine dining

Many of the tips for fast-food and casual dining hold for fine dining as well. However you should expect better quality foods and better attention to your particular needs. Likewise, you can expect to pay more to eat in a fine dining restaurant.

Don't mistake "fine" dining with "healthful" dining. Indeed, the Calories in a poorly selected meal in a fine dining restaurant can easily exceed the Calories in a well-selected meal at an otherwise notoriously high-fat, fast-food restaurant. You have to take control when ordering your meal and have a say in its preparation. Remember that you are the customer.

THE COMPLETE TRAVEL DIET

Restaurant selection

Tip #143 Make reservations
If you have reservations, there will be less of a chance that you will have to hang out in the lounge area with a drink and appetizers waiting for a table. And, if you call during off-peak hours, you can ask to speak to the manager to find out how the meals are prepared and what the portion sizes are. Also inquire if you can get your meal specially prepared (i.e., low-fat).

Food selection

Tip #144 Grill your server (as well as your meal)
A knowledgeable waitperson should be able to answer your questions about how the meals are prepared and what portion sizes are served. If you can't get reliable answers here, ask the manager.

Tip #145 Make your cooking instructions explicit
Instruct your server to take the message to the kitchen that you do not want your food marinated, basted, or brushed with butter or any other oils.

Tip #146 Choose the grade
If you order meat, be aware that the marbling in meat—the component that gives it taste and a tender consistency—is simply fat. The less tender grades of meat are better selections. "Select" grades of meat are lower in fat than are "choice" grades, which in turn have less fat content than "prime" cuts. The words "round," "loin," and "leg" also indicate lower fat cuts of beef, pork, and lamb.

Tip #147 Remove fat
When ordering cuts of meat, tell your server that you want your selection well-trimmed of extra fat *before*

cooking. And make sure your request is noted on your order.

Tip #148 Ask for separate platters
You can best judge correct portion size by having each food item isolated on its own plate rather than bunched with the other items you order.

Tip #149 Request your food be served on smaller dishes
Ask for the serving plates to be down-sized, perhaps child-sized. An appropriate portion size on a small plate looks much more filling than the same size portion on a huge plate.

Tip #150 Skip the dessert selections
At the conclusion of the order taking process, tell your server that if you are going to order dessert at all, it will be fresh fruit. Consequently there is no reason for you to see a dessert menu, so do not bring it to the table. And forget about pushing over a dessert cart.

Meal management

Tip #151 Start with a starch
Most of the foods you eat should come from the starch food group. Consumption of complex carbohydrates found in foods from this group, such as pasta, will make you feel fuller sooner and can curb your desire for higher-fat foods.

Tip #152 Trim the fat
Even though you may have asked that all fat be trimmed away from a meat dish that you ordered, some fat may have been overlooked. So remove whatever fat remains on the edges of your meat selection before you eat it.

THE COMPLETE TRAVEL DIET

Tip #153 Slow down
>Fat is what gives food much of its taste. When eating foods with higher fat content, take more time chewing. Taste every bite.

Tip #154 Enjoy your meal
>If you did your homework and ordered your meal with healthful choices of appropriate portion sizes in mind, there is no reason not to enjoy the taste of your food as well as enjoying the company and surroundings of the restaurant.

Tip #155 Stop when servings have disappeared...
>When you have eaten the allotment of food you have determined as appropriate for the meal, stop eating. Don't wait for the taste to run out or for an immediate sense of fullness. A feeling of fullness can take several minutes after you stop eating until it registers in your brain.

Tip #156 ...or stop when satisfied
>Of course, if you feel satisfied before the food you ordered has disappeared, don't feel at all obligated to finish your meal.

Tip #157 Provide a self-imposed signal that the meal is over
>Order coffee (not a coffee drink) or tea (not an after-dinner drink). And once you have placed that order, stop eating.

After your meal

Tip #158 Have your table cleared as soon as you are finished
>Once you are finished with your meal, have the server clear your table so you will not be tempted to nimble at any food remaining, which is easy to do without even realizing it.

Tip #159 *"Poison" your food*
>If the table is not cleared, make the remaining food unpalatable by pouring salt or other condiments on the remaining food.

Tip #160 *Brush your teeth soon after your meal*
>Giving your teeth a rigorous brushing will take your mind off any desire you may have to continue to eat, and it will prevent you from eating again too soon. The fresh taste in your mouth left by your toothpaste can also provide a satisfying alternative to a sweet.

Tip #161 *Take a walk after your meal*
>Some light movement following your meal will facilitate digestion and will help to shift your thoughts away from food. If you have just completed dinner, one of the best ways to prepare your body for sleep is take an easy, after-dinner stroll.

Lounges and bars

For the most part, there are very few opportunities for finding healthful foods in lounges or bars. Almost anything you put in your mouth—snacks, appetizers, and of course alcohol—will be loaded with Calories. What's worse, the food served is often selected to make you drink more, and the drinks served make you want to munch more—a perilous cycle of high-Calorie consumption.

Tip #162 *Beware of "mini-snacks"*
>Salty bar foods such as crackers, pretzels, and nuts are very high in Calories. Although you are just going to "nibble," you will end up eating much more than you realize. So don't even start.

Tip #163 *Drink sparkling water*
>If you feel that you need something just a little bit fancier than plain old water, drink sparkling water.

This will give you a moderate sense of "having a drink" and will help fill you up too.

Returning home

You are back home after following THE COMPLETE TRAVEL DIET while away on vacation or business. Perhaps you have lost a couple of pounds—at least you haven't gained any—and it turned out not to be so difficult after all. Now, how do you integrate the positive changes you have made in your eating and activity habits while you were away into your everyday life back at home?

This is not a trivial matter. Indeed, most people who are successful at losing weight are unsuccessful at keeping that weight off—not "some" people, "*most*" people.

To continue a process of weight loss and to keep that weight off, you must adopt, on a permanent basis, the changes you made to your eating habits and your exercise routine while on your trip. You can improve your chances of success by adopting a lifelong commitment that includes frequent and regular physical activity of at least moderate intensity, and healthy eating in accordance with the Dietary Guidelines for Americans, emphasizing a reduction in total Calories, a lowered fat consumption, and an increase in vegetables, fruits and whole grains.

If you followed the advice about preparing for your return before you left, reminders of your poor habits and temptations to return to those habits have been minimized, if not eliminated. Take this fresh opportunity to change your at-home diet and to rearrange your activity schedule. If you do not make these new behaviors part of your lifestyle, the weight you lost will almost certainly return.

TRAVEL TIPS

Tip #164 Reconsider your weight loss goal
Sometimes on the way to a weight loss goal, people begin to feel differently about their body weight. As you lose weight, you may discover that your initial goal was off the mark. You may want to adjust your goal to lose more weight, lose less weight, or perhaps to remain at your current weight.

Tip #165 Redo your plans
The plan you made to take you to your weight loss goal while traveling was made with traveling in mind. Now that you are back home, you must re-evaluate and modify that plan for the reality of home life.

Tip #166 Make exercise a priority
You are more likely to keep your weight off if you keep up with regular physical activity. That means that you will need to continue a program of 30 minutes or more of moderate physical activity the day that you return from your trip and every day from there on out.

Figure out how you will get your exercise regardless of your job, family obligations, weather conditions, or whatever else has served as an excuse for you in the past from getting the exercise you need.

Tip #167 Readjust your routine
You don't want to return form a trip, after successfully losing some weight, only to have your exercise routine short-circuited by old habits or excuses. You may even find that the exercise routine you set up before you left is less rigorous than what you are capable of upon your return. Readjust your exercise routine from the one you made up prior to leaving on your trip.

THE COMPLETE TRAVEL DIET

Tip #168 *Transfer your habits*
Hopefully by paying attention to your diet and getting some exercise, you have been able to lose weight or at least been able to maintain it while traveling. Now that you know that it is possible to manage your weight under the variable conditions that traveling requires, you can extend some of the same dietary and exercise practices back to your more stable home turf.

Tip #169 *Replace a bad habit with a healthful one*
Stop doing just one more thing that you shouldn't (such as eating fat-filled desserts), and begin doing just one thing that you should but haven't (such as taking an extra 10 minute walk every day). You will demonstrate that you can control your behavior, you will reinforce the notion that you have the power to change, and you will be making two behavioral changes that will affect your weight.

Tip #170 **Celebrate!**
You've modified some behaviors and demonstrated the discipline necessary to control your weight. Good for you. You deserve congratulations and a celebration. Buy yourself a present, spend more time with your hobby, or simply take a walk with family or friends. You are on your way to better health.

TEN

Resources

If you are interested in learning more about how to lose weight sensibly and to keep that weight off, a number of responsible sources of information are available for free.

Government resources

The U.S. government provides many sources of information on nutrition, health, and weight control. Selected resources are listed here.

Nutrition.gov – Provides a gateway to nutrition information from various federal government agencies.
www.nutrition.gov

National Institutes of Health

MEDLINEplus – Carries news, reports, research, and treatments of weight loss and dieting.
www.nlm.nih.gov/medlineplus/weightlossdieting.html

Obesity Education Initiative of the National Heart, Lung, and Blood Institute – Seeks to reduce the risk of coronary heart disease through weight reduction and physical activity.
Tel: 301-592-8573
www.nhlbi.nih.gov

Weight-control Information Network of the National Institute of Diabetes and Digestive and Kidney Diseases – Assembles and disseminates information on weight control, obesity, and nutritional disorders.
Tel: 877-946-4627
www.niddk.nih.gov/health/nutrit/win.htm

U.S. Department of Agriculture

Center for Nutrition Policy and Promotion – Links scientific research with the nutritional needs of the American public.
www.usda.gov/cnpp

Food and Nutrition Information Center – Collects and disseminates information about food and human nutrition.
Tel: 301-504-5719
www.nal.usda.gov/fnic

U.S. Department of Health and Human Services

Center for Food Safety and Applied Nutrition – Promotes and protects the public's health by ensuring that the nation's food supply is safe, sanitary, wholesome, and honestly labeled.
Tel: 888-463-6332
www.cfsan.fda.gov

RESOURCES

Healthfinder® – Serves as a gateway to health information, including diet, nutrition, healthy lifestyle, and physical activity.
www.healthfinder.gov

National Action Plan on Overweight and Obesity – Presents strategies from the Office of the Surgeon General to prevent and decrease overweight and obesity in the population.
www.surgeongeneral.gov/topics/obesity

National Women's Health Information Center – Contains health information and is a referral center for women.
Tel: 800-994-9662
www.4woman.gov

Other organizations

American Academy of Family Physicians – Offers an online brochure about losing weight and keeping it off.
www.familydoctor.org/healthfacts/197/

American Dietetic Association – Provides food and nutrition information.
Tel: 800-877-1600
www.eatright.org

Airport gyms – Lists gyms, exercise centers, and fitness clubs located in or near airport terminals in the U.S. and Canada.
www.airportgyms.com

American Institute for Cancer Research – Publishes news, research updates, recipes, and tips to help live a healthier, cancer-free life.
Tel: 800-843-8114
www.aicr.org

American Obesity Association – Focuses on changing public policy and perceptions about obesity.
Tel: 202-776-7711
www.obesity.org

THE COMPLETE TRAVEL DIET

International Health, Racquet & Sportsclub Association - displays maps with the location of clubs in given communities.
www.healthclubs.com

National Weight Control Registry – Gathers information from people who have successfully lost weight and kept it off.
Tel: 800-606-6927
www.nwcr.org

You

THE COMPLETE TRAVEL DIET users are the best resource for improving THE COMPLETE TRAVEL DIET. Let us know how much weight you lost and how long you have kept it off. And tell us what worked and what didn't.

Send your comments and experiences to:

> THE COMPLETE TRAVEL DIET
> c/o Applied Psychology Press
> 22 Rincon Court / West
> Santa Cruz, CA 95060-1016
> USA

Or email us at feedback@CompleteTravelDiet.com.

Index

A

Activity index 16
Adolescents 9
Airport gyms 185
Alcohol 50
American Academy of
  Family Physicians 185
American Dietetic
  Association 185
American Heart
  Association 142
American Institute for
  Cancer Research 185
American Obesity
  Association 185
Amino acids 30
Arthritis 64
Aspartame 48
Asthma 64

B

Back pain 70
Basal metabolic rate
  (BMR) 16
Benedict, Francis 16
Beverages 49
Birth control 64
Blood pressure 10
Body Mass Index (BMI) .. 12
Breakfast 67

Breast feeding 9
Bulimia 9

C

Calcium 35, 138
Cancer 8
Carbohydrates 28
Carnegie Institute of
  Washington 16
Center for Food Safety and
  Applied Nutrition 184
Center for Nutrition Policy
  and Promotion 184
Children 9
Cholesterol 10
Coffee 49
Complex carbohydrates ... 29
Convenience drinks 50
Copper 35
Cortisol 67
Cruising 173

D

Daily activity log 86
Daily Calorie log
  .... 86, 99, 117
Daily food log 83
Dairy group 45, 54
Dehydration 154
Department of Health and
  Human Services 41

185

Depression............8, 64, 70
Diabetes............8, 9, 64, 70
Dizziness........................10

E

Endorphins 93
Exchange-type diet..........38

F

Fat replacers 47
Fats...................................31
Fiber..........................34, 48
Fitness level.....................12
Food and Nutrition
  Information Center....184
Food ball..........................56
Food cravings..................93
Food Guide Pyramid.......40
Food stack 57
Fructose...........................29
Fruit group................45, 54

G

Gall bladder disease 8
Glucose............................29

H

Hair loss 10
Harris, Arthur 16
Harris-Benedict formula..16
HDL-cholesterol..............33
Healthfinder..................185
Heart disease 8, 9, 32, 70

Heart-healthy 142
High blood pressure 8

I

Inflammatory bowel
  disease..........................64
Iron...........................35, 138

J

Jordan, Michael...............15
Junk food ball..................58
Junk group...............46, 55

K

Kidney disease 9

L

LDL-cholesterol........32, 33
Linoleic acid 31
Linolenic acid..................31
Lupus 64

M

Meal replacements 63
Medications.................9, 64
MEDLINEplus..............184
Menstrual cycle...............10
Mental health 10
Minerals 35
Monounsaturated fats......33
Muscle tone.....................70

N

National Action Plan
  on Overweight
  and Obesity 185
National Heart, Lung, and
  Blood Institute 13
National Institutes
  of Health 184
National Nutrient
  Database (USDA) 99
National Weight
  Control Registry 186
National Women's Health
  Information Center 185
Net daily Calorie goal 81
Nutrition.gov 183

O

Obesity 9
Obesity Education
  Initiative of the
  National Heart, Lung,
  and Blood Institute 184
One pound rule 39
Osteoarthritis 8
Osteoporosis 70

P

Partially hydrogenated
  fats 33
Phytochemicals 43
Polyunsaturated fats 33
Portions 59
Potassium 35

Pregnancy 9
Protein 30, 138
Protein group 45, 55
Psychiatric disorder 9

R

Running 73

S

Saccharin 48
Safety 9, 140
Saturated fats 32
Schwarzenegger, Arnold . 15
Security 140
Selenium 35
Self-esteem 8, 70
Serotonin 93
Simple carbohydrates 28
Sleep 64, 67
Sleep apnea 8
Snacks 64
Sodium 62
Sorbitol 48
Starch group 43, 53
Stationary bicycle 79
Stress 67, 70, 149
Stroke 8
Sugar substitutes 48
Supplements 63
Sweet tooth 95

T

Tea 49
Type 2 diabetes 8, 70

U

United States Department
of Health and
Human Services 184
United States Department of
Agriculture 41, 99
United States Food and
Drug Administration ... 59
Unsaturated fats 32

V

Vegetable group 44, 54
Vegetarians 137
Vitamins 35, 138

Voluntary Guidelines for
Providers of Weight Loss
Products or Services 10

W

Water 36, 50
Weight-control Information
Network of the National
Institute of Diabetes and
Digestive and Kidney
Diseases 184

Z

Zinc 35, 138

Programs

Applied Psychology provides speakers, briefings, presentations, workshops, and consultation services to corporations, government agencies, and not-for-profit associations. To implement THE COMPLETE TRAVEL DIET in your organization contact:

THE COMPLETE TRAVEL DIET
22 Rincon Court / West
Santa Cruz, California 95060-1016
USA
1-800-492-5050
+1-831-439-0922 (outside USA)

www.CompleteTravelDiet.com

Selected products are also available
through THE COMPLETE TRAVEL DIET Web site.

About the author

Dr. Terry Riley is a psychologist and internationally recognized authority on travel behavior. He is principal of Applied Psychology and author of *Travel Can Be Murder: The business traveler's guide to personal safety* and *C.H.A.R.M. School: Lessons in Customer Hostility And Rage Management*.

Terry also writes *The Errogramme* (www.ErrTravel.com), a monthly syndicated column on travel behavior; *Travel Fox* (www.TravelFox.com), satirical reports of travel news; and *A Mind to Travel* (www.SkyGuide.net) a column on the psychology of travel published by American Express.

Terry lives on the central California coast with his wife and many animals.

Books by Dr. Terry Riley

C.H.A.R.M. School
Lessons in Customer Hostility And Rage Management

Travel Can Be Murder
The business traveler's guide to personal safety

The Complete Travel Diet
On the road guide to taking pounds off

Available online from Amazon.com, through your local bookstore, or from Applied Psychology Press

---

Applied Psychology Press offers a discount for orders of five or more books. To purchase these titles, contact Applied Psychology Press at:

22 Rincon Court / West
Santa Cruz, CA 95060-1016
USA
Tel: +1-831-439-0922
Fax: +1-509-278-7397
Email: press@AppliedPsychology.com